THE
allotment
cookbook
through the year

THE
allotment
cookbook
through the year

EDITOR-IN-CHIEF
Caroline Bretherton

DK

LONDON, NEW YORK, MUNICH,
MELBOURNE, DELHI

Senior Editor Alastair Laing
Project Art Editor William Hicks
Editorial Assistant Roxanne Benson-Mackey
Managing Editor Dawn Henderson
Managing Art Editor Marianne Markham
Senior Creative Nicola Powling
Senior Presentations Creative Caroline de Souza
Production Editor Maria Elia
Production Controller Alice Sykes
Creative Technical Support Sonia Charbonnier

DK INDIA
Senior Editor Chitra Subramanyam
Editor Charis Bhagianathan
Senior Art Editor Neha Ahuja
Designer Heema Sabharwal
Managing Editor Glenda Fernandes
Senior Art Editor (Lead) Navidita Thapa
DTP Manager Sunil Sharma
DTP Designer Tarun Sharma
DTP Operator Sourabh Challariya

Editor Nicola Hodgson
New photography William Reavell

First published in Great Britain in 2011 by
Dorling Kindersley Limited
80 Strand, London WC2R 0RL
Penguin Group (UK)

2 4 6 8 10 9 7 5 3 1
001 – 178300 – Mar/2011

A CIP catalogue record for this book
is available from the British Library.
ISBN 978-1-4053-6265-8

Colour reproduction by Colourscan, Singapore
Printed and bound in Singapore by Tien Wah Press

Discover more at **www.dk.com**

CONTENTS

INTRODUCTION

As a child, I grew up in a house with a large vegetable garden. I would watch endless weekends pass as my parents disappeared down to the bottom of the garden, only to reappear hours later tired, dirty, but happy and, no doubt, clutching a few freshly harvested courgettes or a handful of asparagus spears. Come suppertime in summer, I would be sent off with a colander to crawl, commando-style, under the anti-squirrel netting to pick some strawberries for tea. Such things leave a mark on your character and I found, as I grew older, that I had in turn developed a hankering to grow my own.

Living in a city meant this wasn't going to be so easy, but after a long wait I finally inherited an old, overgrown patch of ground that was soon to become my very own allotment. It may be that you have a large or small kitchen garden, balcony, or even roof terrace, rather than an allotment, but whatever piece of soil you have available, there will be something you'll be able to grow on it.

Growing your own is satisfying in so many ways: the excitement of watching the first young seedlings appear; planting out fledgling plants in pleasingly straight rows; and that particular sense of peace that falls over a garden in the early evening, when you have gone out to water and sit down to survey all your work coming to fruition, the stresses of life a distant memory. You may feel tired and dirty after a long day planting potatoes, but it is a weariness filled with its own sweet sense of satisfaction at a job well done.

By far the most fulfilling part of growing your own is harvesting the crops. I'm never sure whether spring is my favourite season, arriving with its tender young peas and broad beans, first delicate lettuces, and early potatoes. But then there is the florid abundance of high summer, when, no matter how fast you pick them, you'll never be able to keep up with the French beans and courgettes. Summer's swansong must be the tomatoes finally ripening into a myriad of shapes and colours, heralding the onset of autumn with its bulging pumpkins for hardening off and storing, before the taming of the plot begins over winter. It is then that I pull up anything else worth preserving and finally set the garden to order, ready for next year. Brassicas, overwintering broad beans, leeks, garlic, and other hardy crops all wait patiently for the spring when the plot once more comes to life.

Finally, there is the cooking. Having invested so much time and energy in growing your own fruit and vegetables, you'll want to make the best of them. I have included in this book some of my favourite recipes for home-grown crops, whether they be simple, everyday supper dishes helping to use up a glut of produce, or more elaborate meals designed to showcase some treasured harvest. Vegetables can often be sidelined as a support act, but after you have grown them yourself you will want to give them a starring role. Tarts and bakes, stews and salads can all be wonderful vehicles to allow the intense flavours of your freshly harvested crops to shine through.

Every gardener knows that a glut of a certain type of fruit or vegetable is inevitable. Depending on your particular climate, different crops will produce unnervingly high yields and you'll want to make the best of them, both in terms of flavour and lack of waste. Eating the same thing every day for a month could get repetitive, so here I hope you'll find inspiration to see your produce in a new light. Pickling, preserving, and freezing are all good ways to lock the goodness of our gardens away for the lean months of winter, and for that reason you will find many recipes and step-by-step techniques that cover all aspects of preserving too.

I can truthfully say there are few things in life that give me greater pleasure than growing, tending, harvesting, and cooking my own produce. Working with the rhythms of the seasons, both in the garden and the kitchen, and eating food that is grown locally, without the use of chemicals, and practically for free, are all things that I find intensely rewarding and I hope you will, too.

Caroline

SPRING

Asparagus

Peas

Broad beans

Chard

Cauliflowers

Spinach

Lettuce

Rocket

Radishes

Rhubarb

ASPARAGUS

When to pick
Pick asparagus when it is no more than 15cm (6in) high and no thicker than your index finger. Harvest with a sharp knife, cutting just below the surface of the soil.

Eat and store fresh
Best eaten as soon as they are picked, stems can be steamed, boiled, or chargrilled. Wrap in damp kitchen paper and store in the fridge for up to 3 days.

How to preserve
Green asparagus can be preserved in oil, having been steamed or chargrilled first (see pages 38–39).

Freezing options
The flavour of the asparagus is best preserved if it is first chargrilled. It can also be blanched briefly, cooled, and then frozen for up to 9 months.

The effort required to grow asparagus is more than rewarded when you pick your first home-grown stems. This rich classic sauce is an ideal accompaniment for such a regal vegetable.

Chargrilled asparagus
with hollandaise

Serves 4 • **Prep** 10 mins • **Cooking** 10 mins

INGREDIENTS

500g (1lb 2oz) asparagus spears, woody ends removed
1 tbsp extra virgin olive oil
2 tbsp white wine vinegar
4 egg yolks
115g (4oz) butter, melted
sea salt and freshly ground black pepper
juice of ½ lemon

METHOD

1 Heat a griddle pan and brush with the oil. When very hot, add the asparagus and grill for 5–6 minutes, depending on the thickness of the spears, turning once, until lightly charred and just tender.

2 Meanwhile, to make the sauce, heat the vinegar in a small pan and allow to bubble until it reduces by half. Remove from the heat, add 2 tbsp water, and then whisk in the egg yolks one at a time.

3 Return the pan to very low heat and whisk continuously until the mixture is thick and light. Remove from the heat and gradually whisk in the melted butter. Season to taste with salt and pepper and stir in the lemon juice.

4 Divide the asparagus between serving plates and serve with the sauce spooned over.

Much as I love simple steamed asparagus, chargrilling the stems is a good alternative, giving a meatier result. Here, the stronger taste of the griddled asparagus is a great match for a sharp, tangy sheep's cheese or Parmesan.

Chargrilled asparagus
with olive oil and sheep's cheese

Serves 4 • **Prep** 5 mins • **Cooking** 10 mins

INGREDIENTS

500g (1lb 2oz)
    asparagus spears,
    woody ends removed
4 tbsp extra virgin olive oil
2 tbsp balsamic vinegar
    or balsamic glaze
coarse sea salt
hard sheep's cheese or
    Parmesan cheese, grated

METHOD

1 Heat a griddle pan and brush with a little of the olive oil. When very hot, add the asparagus and chargrill for 5–6 minutes, depending on the thickness of the spears, turning once, until tender and bright green.

2 Divide the asparagus between serving plates and drizzle with the remaining olive oil and balsamic vinegar or balsamic glaze. Sprinkle the spears with a few grains of coarse sea salt and scatter over flakes of freshly shaved hard sheep's cheese or Parmesan.

The delicate colour of white asparagus is produced by growing it in the dark, a method known as forcing. Served with a subtly flavoured mayonnaise, it makes a glorious late spring dish.

White asparagus
with herby mayonnaise

Serves 4 as a dip • **Prep** 5 mins • **Cooking** 10 mins

INGREDIENTS

500g (1lb 2oz) white or thick
    green asparagus spears,
    woody ends removed
2 egg yolks
2 tbsp white wine vinegar
1 tsp Dijon mustard
300ml (10fl oz) light olive oil
juice of $1/2$ lemon
sea salt and freshly ground
    black pepper
1 garlic clove, crushed
1 tbsp chopped parsley
1 tbsp chopped tarragon

METHOD

1 Fill a pan with enough water to cover most of the spears but leaving the tips exposed. Bring to the boil and place the spears upright in the boiling water, tied into bundles with string, if preferred. Cover them with a lid, or make a loose tent with foil over the top to cover, but not damage, the tips. Cook for 2–3 minutes until the spears are tender but still with bite.

2 Place the egg yolks, vinegar, and mustard in a food processor, and blend for 1–2 minutes, or until pale and creamy. Alternatively, whisk by hand in a large bowl, using a balloon whisk.

3 With the motor still running, or still whisking by hand, slowly pour in the olive oil. Blend until thick, creamy, and smooth.

4 Spoon the mayonnaise into a bowl and stir in the lemon juice. Season to taste with salt and pepper, and stir in the garlic, parsley, and tarragon. Serve as a dip for the cooked asparagus spears.

A simple way to turn a bunch of asparagus into a substantial supper, the lemon zest and salty capers really bring out the freshness of the ingredients in this easy pasta dish.

Zesty asparagus
and courgette pasta

Serves 4 • **Prep** 10 mins • **Cooking** 20 mins

INGREDIENTS

1 tbsp extra virgin olive oil

1 onion, finely chopped

sea salt

4 small courgettes, 2 diced
    and 2 grated

3 garlic cloves, grated
    or finely chopped

1 bunch fine asparagus spears,
    woody ends removed, and
    each cut into 3 pieces

1 small glass of white wine

1–2 tsp rinsed, dried, and
    chopped capers

zest of 1 lemon

350g (12oz) penne pasta

handful of flat-leaf parsley,
    finely chopped

Parmesan cheese, grated,
    to serve

METHOD

1 Heat the oil in a large frying pan, add the onion and a pinch of salt, and cook over low heat for 5 minutes or until soft and translucent. Add all the courgettes, and cook for 10 minutes or until they have cooked down and softened. Don't allow them to brown.

2 Stir in the garlic and asparagus. Add the wine, raise the heat, and allow to boil for 2–3 minutes. Return it to a simmer, cook for 2–3 minutes more, or until the asparagus has softened. Then remove from the heat and stir in the capers and lemon zest.

3 Meanwhile, cook the pasta in a large pan of boiling, salted water for 10 minutes, or until it is cooked but still has a bit of bite to it. Drain, keeping back a tiny amount of the cooking water. Return the pasta to the pan, add the courgette mixture and parsley, and then toss it together. Sprinkle with Parmesan and serve.

Variation For a richer sauce, add 2–3 tbsp double cream at the same time as you return the pasta to the pan, after draining.

This light, fragrant quiche is ideal served still warm and just set, with a slight wobble. A few stems treated this way will take centre stage as part of an elegant lunch or supper dish.

Asparagus quiche

Serves 4–6 • **Prep** 20 mins, plus chilling • **Cooking** 45 mins

INGREDIENTS

For the pastry

175g (6oz) plain flour

pinch of sea salt

45g (1¹/₂oz) cold lard, diced

45g (1¹/₂oz) cold butter, diced

For the filling

175g (6oz) asparagus
    spears

extra virgin olive oil

115g (4oz) cream cheese

2 tsp chopped thyme

freshly ground black pepper

85g (3oz) mature Cheddar
    cheese, grated

2 eggs

150ml (5fl oz) single cream

sea salt

METHOD

1 Sift the flour and salt into a bowl. Add the fat, and rub in with fingertips until the mixture resembles fine breadcrumbs. Mix with 2 tbsp cold water to form a firm dough. Form the pastry into a ball, wrap it in cling film, and leave it in the fridge to chill for 30 minutes.

2 Preheat the oven to 200°C (400°F/Gas 6). Remove the pastry from the fridge and unwrap it. Roll it out in a circle a little larger than a 20cm (8in) loose-bottomed tart tin. Line the tart tin with the pastry. Line the pastry case with greaseproof paper and fill with baking beans. Bake for 10 minutes. Remove the paper and beans, and bake for another 5 minutes. Remove from the oven. Lower the oven temperature to 180°C (350°F/Gas 4).

3 Toss the asparagus in a little olive oil. Cook on a hot griddle pan for 2 minutes on each side. Spread the cream cheese over the pastry case. Sprinkle with the thyme, some pepper, and the Cheddar cheese. Trim the asparagus spears to fit, scatter the trimmings over the cheese and lay the spears on top. Beat the eggs and cream together with a little salt and pepper. Pour into the pastry case. Bake in the oven for about 30 minutes, until golden and just set. Serve warm or cold.

PEAS

When to pick
Peas should be picked frequently to encourage regrowth. Choose small, tender peas if eating the whole pod, or leave the pod to swell if harvesting only the peas inside.

Eat and store fresh
Peas should always be eaten as soon as possible after harvesting, as the natural sugars in the vegetable soon turn to starch.

How to preserve
Larger peas can be dried for winter cooking (see page 93), or the whole pods used to make pea pod wine.

Freezing options
Peas freeze well. Blanch for 1–2 minutes, leave to cool, then open freeze on trays, bag up, and store in the freezer for up to 12 months.

Growing peas is one of the greatest pleasures, but discarding the pods can sometimes seem like such a waste. Here, the pods as well as the peas can be used to make this vibrant spring soup.

Pea soup
with mint gremolata

Serves 6 • **Prep** 10 mins • **Cooking** 35 mins

INGREDIENTS

30g (1oz) butter

1 onion, finely chopped

1 potato, roughly chopped

550g (1¼lb) peas in their
    pods, roughly cut up

1.2 litres (2 pints) chicken
    or vegetable stock

1 tsp caster sugar

sprig of mint

sea salt and freshly ground
    black pepper

single cream, to serve

For the gremolata

2 tbsp finely chopped
    flat-leaf parsley

2 tbsp finely chopped mint

2 tsp finely grated lemon zest

1 garlic clove, finely chopped

METHOD

1 Melt the butter in a pan, add the onion, and cook gently over low heat, stirring until softened (about 7–10 minutes). Add the remaining soup ingredients, apart from the cream. Bring to the boil, reduce the heat, part-cover, and simmer gently for 20 minutes until the peas and potato are really soft. Discard the mint.

2 Purée the soup in a food processor or using a hand-held blender. Pass through a sieve to remove any tough bits of pod and pea skins. Taste and season again, if necessary. Reheat to serve.

3 Meanwhile, thoroughly mix together the gremolata ingredients. Ladle the soup into bowls. Add a swirl of cream and sprinkle with a little gremolata.

This classic Spanish tapas dish is a good way to use peas that have grown a little larger, as their slightly mealy texture stands up to the strong flavours of Serrano ham and smoked paprika.

Spanish-style peas with ham

Serves 4 • **Prep** 5 mins • **Cooking** 15 mins

INGREDIENTS

2 tbsp extra virgin olive oil

1 onion, finely chopped

200g (7oz) Serrano ham, diced

200ml (7fl oz) passata or
   sieved tomatoes

1 tsp sweet paprika

500g (1lb 2oz) peas

1 garlic clove, crushed

1 tbsp finely chopped parsley

2 tsp sea salt

150ml (5fl oz) dry white wine

freshly ground black pepper

METHOD

1 Heat the oil in a frying pan over medium heat and add the onion. Fry for 5 minutes, stirring frequently, until soft.

2 Increase the heat, add the ham, and fry until it begins to brown, then add the tomatoes and sweet paprika. Bring to boiling point, reduce the heat, and simmer for 3 minutes, stirring frequently. Stir in the peas.

3 Mix together the garlic, parsley, and salt, then stir in the wine. Pour this mixture into the pan, and season to taste with pepper. Simmer for 5 minutes, transfer to a heated serving dish, and serve hot.

Baby peas can here be shown at their absolute best, added raw to this delicate salad. To make a main course dish, substitute the feta for some slabs of hot or cold grilled salmon.

Pea and feta salad
with watercress mayonnaise

Serves 4 • **Prep** 15 mins

INGREDIENTS

handful of watercress, roughly chopped

3–4 tbsp good-quality mayonnaise

1 tsp creamed horseradish

salt and freshly ground black pepper

175g (6oz) feta cheese, cubed

125g (4½oz) peas

2 handfuls of baby spinach leaves

small handful of mint leaves

lemon wedges, to serve

METHOD

1 Using a food processor, whiz the watercress, mayonnaise, and creamed horseradish until well combined. Season with salt and black pepper to taste.

2 Put the feta, peas, spinach, and mint leaves in a bowl, and gently combine. Season with a little pepper if you wish. Transfer to a serving bowl, and serve with the mayonnaise and lemon wedges on the side.

Note If it's not the season for fresh peas, frozen ones make an ideal substitute. Leave them to defrost in a bowl, then pour over boiling water, and leave for about 5 minutes. Drain and refresh with cold water. You could use a good-quality fresh ricotta cheese instead of the feta. If you do, omit the mayonnaise mixture.

A deceptively simple dish to prepare, this recipe showcases late spring produce. The bright colours of the peas and asparagus contrast beautifully with the golden yolk of the poached egg.

Warm pea pancakes
with chargrilled asparagus

Serves 4 (makes 8 pancakes) • **Prep** 10 mins • **Cooking** 30 mins

INGREDIENTS

400g (14oz) fresh peas, podded weight

1 large handful of mint leaves, chopped

50g (1³/₄oz) melted butter, plus extra for frying

4 tbsp plain flour

4 tbsp double cream

2 tbsp Parmesan cheese, grated

6 large eggs

sea salt and freshly ground black pepper

1 large bunch of asparagus spears, woody ends removed

1 tsp extra virgin olive oil

METHOD

1 Put the peas in a pan and blanch in boiling water for 1–2 minutes, then drain and leave to cool.

2 Put the peas and mint into a food processor and whizz together to get a rough texture. Add the melted butter, flour, cream, Parmesan, 2 eggs, and season with salt and pepper. Process the mixture to a stiff paste.

3 Heat some butter or oil in a large frying pan and add a couple of tablespoonfuls of the mixture for each pancake. Cook over medium heat, and use the back of a spoon to smooth the top of the mixture. After 3–4 minutes, the edges of the pancakes will change colour. Carefully turn them over and cook for another couple of minutes.

4 Meanwhile, bring a large pan of water to a boil and lightly poach the remaining eggs until just set. Remove them with a slotted spoon.

5 As the eggs are cooking, chargrill the asparagus in a hot griddle pan with a little olive oil, seasoning while cooking, until golden.

BROAD BEANS

When to pick

Harvest beans when the pods are firm and swollen. Pick from the bottom of the plant upwards. Young bean pods can be picked and eaten whole.

Eat and store fresh

Eat as soon as possible if eating raw or whole. The podded beans will keep for 2–3 days in a plastic bag in the fridge.

How to preserve

The beans can be dried for winter use. Remove from the pod and air dry on a rack (see page 93).

Freezing options

Blanch the beans for 2 minutes and cool. Peel them and freeze in small portions for up to 12 months.

Inspired by the classic Italian bread salad, panzanella, this unusual green version is redolent of the fresh colours and flavours of spring, cut with the salty tang of crumbled feta.

Broad bean
and feta panzanella

Serves 4 • **Prep** 25 mins, plus standing • **Cooking** 10 mins

INGREDIENTS

400g (14oz) freshly podded broad beans

150g (5½oz) ciabatta diced into 2cm (¾in) cubes

180ml (6fl oz) extra virgin olive oil

sea salt and freshly ground black pepper

2 tbsp white wine vinegar

1 large garlic clove, crushed

4 spring onions, green parts removed, and finely chopped

200g (7oz) feta cheese, diced into 1cm (½in) cubes or roughly crumbled

1 handful of mint, chopped

2 tbsp chopped dill (optional)

4 handfuls of rocket, watercress, or baby lettuce leaves

juice of 1 lemon

METHOD

1 Preheat the oven to 220°C (425°F/Gas 7). Cook the beans in boiling salted water for 2–3 minutes until just cooked, then plunge them into cold water to cool them and peel off the skins.

2 Meanwhile toss the diced bread in 4 tablespoons of olive oil, sprinkle with a little salt and pepper, and cook at the top of the hot oven for about 8 minutes, turning once, until the bread is golden brown and crispy.

3 In a large serving bowl, whisk together the remaining olive oil, vinegar, and garlic, then season with plenty of black pepper and just a little salt (the feta is salty). Add the broad beans, toasted bread, chopped spring onions, feta, and herbs, and toss well to coat everything.

4 Leave the salad for 30 minutes to develop the flavours and soften the bread. To serve, add the salad leaves, squeeze the lemon over, and check again for seasoning.

Only the tiniest broad beans can be left in their skins, all others should be peeled first before crushing to make this vividly coloured, nutritious, and delicious snack or starter.

Broad bean crostini
with tarragon

Serves 4 (makes 12) • **Prep** 15 mins • **Cooking** 15 mins

INGREDIENTS

½ baguette

3 tbsp extra virgin olive oil

sea salt and freshly ground
     black pepper

100g (3½oz) broad beans,
     podded weight

1 small shallot

1 garlic clove

small bunch of tarragon

METHOD

1 Preheat the oven to 150°C (300°F/Gas 2). Slice the baguette into 12 thin slices and brush both sides with 2 tbsp of the olive oil. Season with salt and pepper. Place flat on a baking tray and bake for 15 minutes, or until crisp all the way through.

2 Meanwhile, blanch the beans in a pan of boiling water for 2 minutes, drain, and refresh in cold water. Remove the tough outer skins and discard. Remove a few beans for garnish and place the remainder in a food processor with the shallot, garlic, remaining olive oil, and tarragon. Process to form a thick paste. Season to taste with salt and pepper.

3 Spread onto the prepared crostini just before serving. Garnish with the reserved beans and a sprinkling of pepper.

Chard is a marvellous plant that can be substituted for spinach in most recipes. Take care to remove the central ribs, which need to be cooked longer than the more delicate leaves.

Chard and Gruyère tart

Serves 6 • **Prep** 15 mins • **Cooking** up to 1 hour 20 mins, plus cooling

INGREDIENTS

300g (10½oz) ready-made
  shortcrust pastry

plain flour, for dusting

2 eggs, plus 1 extra, lightly
  beaten, for egg wash

1 tbsp extra virgin olive oil

1 onion, finely chopped

sea salt and freshly ground
  black pepper

2 garlic cloves, grated
  or finely chopped

few sprigs of rosemary, leaves
  picked and finely chopped

250g (9oz) chard, stalks
  trimmed and leaves
  roughly chopped

125g (4½oz) Gruyère cheese,
  grated

125g (4½oz) feta cheese,
  cubed

200ml (7fl oz) double cream
  or whipping cream

METHOD

1 Preheat the oven to 200°C (400°F/Gas 6). On a surface dusted with flour, roll out the pastry in a circle large enough to fit a loose-bottomed 23cm (9in) tart tin. Trim away the excess, line the pastry shell with greaseproof paper, and fill with baking beans. Bake in the oven for 15–30 minutes until the edges are golden. Remove the beans and paper, and brush the bottom of the shell with a little of the egg wash. Return to the oven for 1–2 minutes to crisp up, then set aside. Reduce the oven temperature to 180°C (350°F/Gas 4).

2 Heat the oil in a pan over low heat. Add the onion and a pinch of salt, and sweat for 5 minutes, until soft. Add the garlic and rosemary, and cook for a few seconds, then add the chard. Stir for 5 minutes until it wilts.

3 Spoon the onion and chard mixture into the pastry shell. Sprinkle over the Gruyère cheese, and scatter evenly with the feta. Season well with salt and pepper. Mix together the cream and the 2 eggs until well combined, and carefully pour over the tart filling. Bake in the oven for 30–40 minutes until set and golden. Leave to cool for 10 minutes before releasing from the tin. Serve warm or at room temperature.

CHARD

When to pick
Pick chard at any stage. Cut the leaves 2–3cm (¾–1¼in) above the base. Tiny leaves can be eaten raw, the bigger ones cooked. Cook the central ribs separately.

Eat and store fresh
Baby chard is best used immediately if eaten raw. The bigger leaves can be washed, dried, and kept in a plastic bag in the fridge, for up to 3 days.

Freezing options
Wash and shred the leaves, blanch for 1–2 minutes, cool, squeeze out excess water, and then freeze for up to 12 months.

This rich, warming dish uses only the dark green leaves of chard, but rather than simply discarding the often colourful stems, cut them into lengths, steam for a few minutes, and serve alongside.

Gratin of chard
with haricots and pancetta

Serves 4–6 • **Prep** 10 mins, plus soaking • **Cooking** 1 hour 20 mins, plus resting

INGREDIENTS

400g (14oz) dried haricot
   or canellini beans,
   soaked overnight
200g (7oz) pancetta, diced
2 tbsp extra virgin olive oil
4 garlic cloves, crushed
400g (14oz) chard, destalked
   and finely shredded
600ml (1 pint) double cream
sea salt and freshly ground
   black pepper
100g (3½oz) white bread
60g (2oz) Parmesan
   cheese, grated
8 basil leaves

METHOD

1 Preheat the oven to 200°C (400°F/Gas 6). Drain the soaked beans, put them in a large pan of water, and bring to a boil. Turn down to a strong simmer and skim off any foam that has collected on the surface. Continue to cook for around 40 minutes, or until soft.

2 In another large, deep-sided pan, cook the pancetta in the olive oil for 3–4 minutes until it is golden brown. Add the garlic and continue to cook for up to 30 seconds, being careful not to burn the garlic. Remove the garlic and pancetta from the oil and set aside. Add the chard to the oil in the pan and cook, stirring, for about 1 minute until it has collapsed, but is still *al dente*.

3 Add the pancetta, garlic, and cooked beans to the chard. Mix well, stir in the cream, and season.

4 Tip everything into a 1.5 litre (2¾ pint) gratin dish. Top with breadcrumbs made by whizzing up the white bread, Parmesan, and basil in a food processor. Cook at the top of the oven for 30 minutes until golden brown. Leave the gratin to rest for 10 minutes before serving.

CAULIFLOWERS

When to pick
Pick cauliflowers when the heads are no bigger than 15–20cm (6–8in) across, and the florets are tight and firm. Cut the stem 5cm (2in) below the head.

Eat and store fresh
Young cauliflower that is to be eaten raw should be used as soon as possible. Store larger heads, with the inner leaves intact, in the fridge for up to 5 days.

How to preserve
Use cauliflowers in chutneys, pickles, and relishes (see pages 36–7), or preserve them in oil (see pages 38–9).

Freezing options
Separate into florets, blanch for 3 minutes, then cool and freeze for up to 12 months.

The mildness of cauliflower works wonderfully with the subtle spiciness of toasted coriander seeds here. The bacon may be omitted for a simpler, vegetarian version.

Cauliflower soup
with toasted coriander

Serves 4–6 • **Prep** 15–20 mins • **Cooking** 40 mins

INGREDIENTS

2 tsp coriander seeds
40g (1½oz) unsalted butter
1 onion, chopped
1 potato, chopped
1 head of cauliflower,
    outer leaves removed,
    separated into small florets
salt and freshly ground
    black pepper
500ml (16fl oz)
    vegetable stock
1 bay leaf
8 streaky bacon rashers,
    rinds removed
200ml (7fl oz) milk
100ml (3½fl oz) single cream

METHOD

1 Heat a heavy-based frying pan or small griddle pan and lightly toast the coriander seeds, stirring all the time, for about a minute. Grind the seeds to a coarse powder using a mortar and pestle, and set aside.

2 Melt the butter in a large pan over low heat. Add the onion and potato, cover, and leave to soften for 10 minutes. Add the cauliflower and ground coriander, season well, cover, and continue cooking for another 10 minutes.

3 Pour over the stock, add the bay leaf, cover, and simmer for about 15 minutes, until the cauliflower has softened. Meanwhile, cook the bacon rashers under a hot grill until crisp. Drain on kitchen paper, roughly chop, and set aside.

4 Remove the bay leaf and blend the soup to a purée with a hand-held blender or in a liquidizer. Stir in the milk and add the cream. Reheat and season again if necessary. Ladle the soup into bowls and scatter with the chopped bacon before serving.

There is nothing more comforting than a good, old-fashioned cauliflower cheese. The secret is to boil or steam the cauliflower until just *al dente* and finish the cooking in the oven.

Cauliflower cheese

Serves 4–6 • **Prep** 15 mins • **Cooking** 15 mins

INGREDIENTS

1 head of cauliflower, outer
    leaves removed, separated
    into large florets
30g (1oz) butter, diced
3 tbsp plain white
    or wholemeal flour
1$\frac{1}{2}$ tsp mustard powder
450ml (15fl oz) milk
125g (4$\frac{1}{2}$oz) mature Cheddar
    cheese, grated
sea salt and freshly ground
    black pepper
100g (3$\frac{1}{2}$oz) fresh
    breadcrumbs

METHOD

1 Bring a large pan of salted water to a boil. Add the cauliflower florets and boil for 7 minutes, or until just tender. Drain well and rinse with cold water to stop the cooking. Arrange the florets in an ovenproof serving dish.

2 Preheat the grill to its highest setting. To make the cheese sauce, melt the butter in a pan over low heat, add the flour and mustard powder, and stir to combine. Cook for 2 minutes, stirring all the time. Remove from the heat, add the milk, and stir constantly until smooth. Return to the heat and bring slowly to a boil. Then reduce the heat and simmer to thicken for 1–2 minutes.

3 Remove the pan from the heat and stir in three-quarters of the cheese until it melts. Season to taste with salt and pepper, and then pour the sauce over the florets.

4 Toss the remaining cheese with the breadcrumbs and sprinkle over the florets. Place the dish under the grill for 10 minutes, or until the sauce bubbles and the top is golden. Serve hot.

A few spices can turn the humble cauliflower into something far more interesting. This dish can be served simply with some buttery basmati rice, or as part of an Indian meal.

Braised cauliflower
with chilli and coriander

Serves 4 • **Prep** 10 mins • **Cooking** 10 mins

INGREDIENTS

400g (14oz) cauliflower,
   outer leaves removed,
   chopped into small florets
2 dried red chillies
1 tsp cumin seeds
2 tbsp sunflower oil
1 tsp black mustard seeds
1/2 tsp turmeric
2 garlic cloves, crushed
knob of butter
sea salt
2 tbsp finely chopped coriander

METHOD

1 Blanch the cauliflower in salted boiling water for 1–2 minutes, drain, and rinse under cold water.

2 Grind together the chillies and cumin seeds in a mortar and pestle, until roughly broken down. Heat the sunflower oil in a large, deep-sided frying pan or wok, and add the chilli and cumin seeds, mustard seeds, turmeric, and garlic. Cook gently for 1 minute until the mustard seeds start to pop.

3 Add the cauliflower and enough water so that it covers the bottom of the pan (about 6 tbsp). Bring the water to a boil and cover the pan or wok. Turn the heat down and simmer the cauliflower for 3–5 minutes, until almost cooked through.

4. Uncover the pan or wok and turn up the heat. Allow the water to cook off, turning the cauliflower all the time. When all the water has evaporated (about 5–6 minutes), add the butter and mix well until it melts. Season with salt and sprinkle with coriander, before serving.

This vibrant yellow pickle is given its colour by a combination of turmeric and mustard powder. It is a classic accompaniment to cold, cooked ham, or hard cheeses such as Cheddar.

Piccalilli

Makes 2.25kg (5lb) or 3 medium jars • **Prep** 15 mins, plus soaking • **Cooking** 20 mins

INGREDIENTS

1 head of cauliflower, outer
    leaves removed, separated
    into small florets
2 large onions, quartered,
    and finely sliced,
    or small pickling onions
900g (2lb) mixed vegetables,
    such as courgettes, runner
    beans, carrots, and
    French beans, cut into
    bite-sized pieces
60g (2oz) sea salt
2 tbsp plain flour
225g (8oz) granulated sugar
    (increase this quantity
    slightly if you don't like
    the pickle too sharp)
1 tbsp turmeric
60g (2oz) English
    mustard powder
900ml (1$\frac{1}{2}$ pints) ready-spiced
    pickling vinegar

METHOD

1 Put all the vegetables in a large non-metallic bowl. Dissolve the salt in 1.2 litres (2 pints) water and pour this brine over the vegetables. Put a plate on top and keep the vegetables submerged for 24 hours.

2 Drain the vegetables and rinse in cold water, then add them to a large pan of boiling water, and blanch for about 2 minutes. Do not overcook them: they should still retain some crunch. Drain and refresh in cold water.

3 Put the flour, sugar, turmeric, and mustard powder in a small bowl and mix in a little of the vinegar to make a paste. Put it in a large stainless steel pan along with the remaining vinegar, bring to a boil, and stir continuously so no lumps appear. Reduce the heat and simmer for about 15 minutes.

4 Add the vegetables to the sauce and stir well so they are coated. Ladle into warm, sterilized jars with non-metallic or vinegar-proof lids, making sure there are no air gaps, before sealing and labelling.

Note Store in a cool, dark place. Allow the flavours to mature for at least 1 month, and refrigerate after opening. Unopened it will keep for 6 months.

Preserve vegetables in oil

Traditionally, many vegetables, olives, and cheeses were stored under olive oil. These days, this technique is considered a short-term method of preservation, and produce stored in this way should always be refrigerated. When preserving vegetables in oil, they are first cooked in vinegar to acidify them, before being covered in oil and refrigerated. Once opened, top up with extra oil, to keep the vegetables covered. Serve with torn basil leaves or chopped parsley, and bread.

1 **Dice or slice** Wash and peel the vegetables as necessary and cut into even-sized pieces about 1cm (½in) thick. Leave small shallots and mushrooms whole.

2 **Add to the pan** Put the vegetables in batches in a stainless steel saucepan and add enough vinegar to just cover them. Add the sugar and salt and bring to a boil.

Recipe Mixed vegetables

Makes approx. 675g (1¹/₂lb) or 2 medium jars
Prep 20 mins • **Cooking** 10 mins • **Keeps** 1–2 months

INGREDIENTS

600g (1lb 5oz) vegetables
white wine vinegar
2 tsp caster sugar
2 tsp sea salt
150ml (5fl oz) extra virgin
  olive oil

for seasonings choose from:
1 tsp dried fennel seeds,
1 tsp dried oregano, 1 fresh
or dried bay leaf, 1 sprig
rosemary, 1 sprig lemon
thyme, pinch of chilli flakes

Other vegetables to try

Mediterranean vegetables are particularly suited to this method of preservation, but other vegetables work well too.

Asparagus Preserve the green variety.
Fennel The crunchy texture and aniseed flavour lends itself to storing in oil.
Garlic Cook and store as whole cloves or purée.
Globe artichokes Chargrilled baby artichokes are particularly good (see page 81).
Peppers Choose ripe, firm, unblemished peppers.
Tomatoes Oven-dry first (see pages 92–3).

3 **Boil and reserve** Boil soft vegetables 2–3 minutes and boil firmer vegetables until *al dente*, then pat dry on kitchen paper and allow to cool.

4 **Store under oil** Pack the vegetables into sterilized jars, add the seasonings, cover with olive oil, and press down lightly. Top up with oil, seal, and store in the fridge.

When to pick
Pick spinach at any time, cutting the leaves 2–3cm (³/₄–1¹/₄in) above the base. Used as a "cut and come again" vegetable, a few plants should last until the first frosts.

Eat and store fresh
Baby spinach is lovely when eaten raw in salads straight from picking. Wash and dry larger leaves and keep in a plastic bag in the fridge for up to 3 days.

Freezing options
Wash and shred the leaves, blanch for 1–2 minutes, leave to cool, squeeze out excess water, and then freeze for up to 12 months.

With this fragrant and vividly coloured soup, the spinach is added at the last moment so that it does not overcook and lose any of the colour or flavour that are such a vital part of the dish.

Creamy spinach
and rosemary soup

Serves 6 • Prep 15 mins • Cooking 25 mins

INGREDIENTS

50g (1³/₄oz) butter
110g (4oz) finely
    chopped onion
150g (5¹/₂oz) diced potato
sea salt and freshly ground
    black pepper
450ml (15fl oz) hot vegetable
    stock, chicken stock,
    or water
450ml (15fl oz) creamy milk,
    made from 335ml (11fl oz)
    whole milk mixed with
    115ml (4fl oz) single cream
350g (12oz) spinach, destalked,
    rinsed, and roughly chopped
1 tbsp chopped rosemary
2 tbsp single cream, to garnish
sprig of rosemary and
    rosemary flowers, to garnish

METHOD

1 Melt the butter in a heavy pan. When it starts to foam, add the onion and potato, and stir to coat well. Season well with salt and freshly ground black pepper, then cover the pan with a lid and sweat the vegetables over gentle heat for 10 minutes.

2 Add the stock and milk, bring to a boil, then simmer for 5 minutes or until the potato and onion are completely cooked. Add the spinach and boil the soup with the lid removed for 2–3 minutes or until tender. Do not overcook. Add the chopped rosemary, then whizz the soup in a food processor or using a hand-held blender, until smooth. Return to the pan and reheat gently.

3 Serve in warm bowls garnished with a swirl of cream and a sprig of rosemary. If you have a rosemary bush in bloom, sprinkle a few flowers over the top for extra pizzazz. This is good with crusty bread or cheese scones.

This mild, creamy curry, flavoured with coconut, is perfect for using up a glut of tomatoes and spinach from your allotment. It makes a light and fragrant supper dish that is easy to prepare.

Spinach and coconut
prawn curry

Serves 4 • **Prep** 15 mins • **Cooking** 20 mins

INGREDIENTS

2 tbsp sunflower oil

2 red onions, finely chopped

4 garlic cloves, finely chopped

large thumb-sized knob of
    ginger, finely grated

$\frac{1}{4}$–$\frac{1}{2}$ tsp chilli powder

$\frac{1}{2}$ tsp turmeric

2 tsp ground cumin

1 tsp ground coriander

4 large tomatoes, skinned
    and finely chopped

400ml (14fl oz) coconut milk

10 fresh or dried curry
    leaves (optional)

150g (5$\frac{1}{2}$oz) spinach, rinsed,
    stalks removed, and leaves
    finely shredded

400g (14oz) raw king prawns,
    shelled weight

$\frac{1}{2}$ tsp caster sugar

sea salt

METHOD

1 Heat the sunflower oil in a large, deep-sided frying pan or wok. Add the onions, garlic, and ginger and cook for 2–3 minutes over low heat until softened, but not brown. Add the spices and cook for a further 1–2 minutes to release the flavours.

2 Add the tomatoes and continue to cook over low heat for another 2 minutes, until the flesh starts to break down. Add the coconut milk and curry leaves (if using), and bring to a boil. Mix in the spinach and lower the heat, continuing to cook until the spinach has collapsed. Baby spinach will take 1–2 minutes, bigger leaves up to 4 minutes.

3 Add the prawns, sugar, and a pinch of salt, and cook for a further 2 minutes over high heat, or until the prawns turn a bright pink colour. Serve with basmati rice, naan bread, and lime wedges on the side.

Growing spinach is both easy and rewarding. If you tire of eating it simply wilted down in olive oil, butter, and garlic, try making these delightful little soufflés instead.

Spinach soufflés

Serves 4 • **Prep** 20 mins • **Cooking** 25–30 mins

INGREDIENTS

225g (8oz) spinach, destalked, rinsed, and roughly chopped
45g (1½oz) butter, plus extra for greasing
45g (1½oz) plain flour
360ml (12fl oz) milk
75g (2½oz) Parmesan cheese, grated
pinch of grated nutmeg
sea salt and freshly ground black pepper
4 large eggs, separated

METHOD

1 Preheat the oven to 200°C (400°F/Gas 6). Cook the spinach, covered, in a large pan over medium heat for 2–3 minutes or until wilted. Drain, squeezing out as much excess water as possible.

2 Butter 4 x 200ml (7fl oz) ramekins and place on a baking tray in the oven. Melt the rest of the butter in a pan and add the flour. Cook gently for a minute, then gradually add the milk, whisking all the time. Bring to a boil, then reduce the heat and leave to simmer for 3–4 minutes. Reserve 2 tbsp of the Parmesan and add the rest to the pan, along with the nutmeg, and season to taste with salt and pepper. Transfer the cheese sauce to a large bowl.

3 Stir the spinach into the mixture. Leave it to cool, then stir in the egg yolks. Whisk the egg whites until stiff and stir 2 tbsp of these into the sauce, before folding in the remainder.

4 Carefully spoon the mixture into the preheated ramekins. Run a knife around the edge of the mixture to help the soufflés rise neatly. Sprinkle with the reserved Parmesan and bake in the preheated oven for 20–25 minutes, or until well-risen and golden. Serve immediately.

Here the bitter taste of frisée lettuce is offset by the saltiness of smoked bacon and the unctuous texture of a perfectly poached egg. Other firm-leaved and crunchy lettuces may be used.

Bistro salad
with egg and lardons

Serves 4 • **Prep** 5 mins • **Cooking** 10 mins

INGREDIENTS

4 eggs

1 tbsp lemon juice

6 tbsp extra virgin olive oil

2 thick slices of bread

1 garlic clove, halved

5mm (¼in) slice fresh root
    ginger (optional)

115g (4oz) smoked lardons

½–1 frisée lettuce, torn

3 sprigs of thyme, leaves picked

small handful of flat-leaf parsley

small handful of coriander

1 small red onion, thinly sliced

For the dressing

2 tbsp red wine vinegar

¼ tsp dried chilli flakes

2 tsp Worcestershire sauce

¼ tsp caster sugar

sea salt and freshly ground
    black pepper

METHOD

1 Poach the eggs in gently simmering water with the lemon juice for about 3 minutes. Scoop out, and put straight into cold water.

2 Remove the crusts from the bread and discard them. Dice the bread. Heat 1 tbsp olive oil in a non-stick frying pan. Add the bread, garlic, and ginger (if using), tossing and stirring until golden. Drain the croutons on kitchen paper. Discard the garlic and ginger.

3 In the same pan, dry-fry the lardons until crisp and golden. Drain on kitchen paper.

4 Put the lettuce in a salad bowl, and tear in the herbs. Add the onion, separated into rings, lardons, and croutons.

5 Add the remaining 5 tbsp olive oil to a pan with the dressing ingredients. Heat gently, stirring. Pour over the salad and toss. Arrange the salad into individual bowls and top each with a poached egg.

LETTUCE

When to pick
Pick leaves when young, glossy, and crisp-looking, picking the outer leaves first. Harvest when the heart is large but firm. "Cut and come again" varieties can be harvested as needed.

Eat and store fresh
Eat as soon as possible for the sweetest flavour. Keep individual heads, unwashed, in the fridge for up to 3 days. "Cut and come again" leaves can be washed, dried, and stored in a plastic bag for up to 3 days in the fridge.

This chilled soup recipe is a wonderful way to use up excess lettuce, but remember only to use the sweetest lettuces to emphasise the flavour of this delicate vegetable.

Lettuce soup
with peas

Serves 4 • **Prep** 20 mins, plus 30 mins chilling

INGREDIENTS

125g (4$^{1}/_{2}$oz) peas
   (shelled weight)
1 small garlic clove
pinch of coarse salt
2 medium round lettuces,
   about 500g (1lb 2oz) in
   total, cleaned, torn into
   pieces, and solid cores
   discarded
250ml (8fl oz) plain yogurt
2cm ($^{3}/_{4}$in) piece fresh ginger,
   peeled and finely grated
handful of mint leaves
juice of $^{1}/_{2}$ lemon
sea salt and freshly ground
   black pepper

METHOD

1 Bring a small amount of water to a boil in a pan, add the peas, and cook for 1 minute. Drain, reserving the cooking water, cool under cold running water, and refrigerate.

2 Cut the garlic in half, remove any green at the centre and discard. Crush with the salt.

3 Combine the garlic with all the other ingredients (except the peas) in a food processor or blender, adding just enough of the reserved cooking water to get the blades moving or until the desired consistency is achieved. This will vary according to the type of lettuce and the kind of machine you are using, but aim to get it fairly smooth, with a bit of texture.

4 Transfer the soup to a large bowl and chill for 30 minutes. When ready to serve, stir through the cooked peas, leaving a few to garnish.

A mix of lettuce varieties and spicy leaves, such as rocket or mizuna, really lifts this salad. If you have been preserving your artichoke hearts in oil (see p81), this is an ideal time to use them.

Antipasti salad

Serves 4 • **Prep** 30 mins • **Cooking** 10 mins

INGREDIENTS

400g (14oz) French beans
sea salt and freshly ground
   black pepper
3 tbsp chopped parsley
2 tsp lemon thyme leaves
1 tbsp chopped fennel fronds
2 tbsp extra virgin olive oil
125g (4½oz) mixed lettuce
   and spicy salad leaves
400g jar of artichoke hearts
4 slices Parma ham
16 black olives, pitted
   and chopped
125g (4½oz) cherry tomatoes
2 spring onions, chopped
3 tbsp chopped chervil

For the dressing

5 tbsp extra virgin olive oil
sea salt and freshly ground
   black pepper
½ garlic clove, crushed
1½ tbsp balsamic vinegar

METHOD

1 Bring a pan of lightly salted water to a boil. Top and tail the French beans and blanch in the boiling water for 5–7 minutes. Refresh in cold water and drain.

2 Place the beans in a wide, shallow salad bowl. Season lightly with salt and pepper and scatter over half the parsley, lemon thyme, and fennel. Drizzle over the olive oil, toss, and set aside.

3 Make the dressing by pouring the olive oil into a small jug. Season with salt and pepper, and then whisk in the garlic and balsamic vinegar.

4 Scatter the salad leaves over the beans, then the drained and halved artichoke hearts, thinly shredded ham, olives, halved tomatoes, and spring onions. Whisk the dressing and drizzle it over the salad. Toss, sprinkle over the chervil, and serve.

This is a wonderfully light and zesty salad. Fresh crabmeat is combined with the sweet and sour flavour of pink grapefruit, and finished with coriander leaves.

Crab salad
with grapefruit

Serves 4 • **Prep** 10 mins

INGREDIENTS

350g (12oz) cooked fresh
    or canned white
    crabmeat, drained
handful of baby salad leaves
handful of coriander leaves
2 pink grapefruits, peeled,
    segmented, pith removed

For the dressing

3 tbsp extra virgin olive oil
1 tbsp white wine vinegar
pinch of caster sugar
sea salt and freshly ground
    black pepper

METHOD

1 In a small bowl or jug, whisk together the dressing ingredients. Season with salt and pepper.

2 Mix the crabmeat with a drizzle of the dressing. Divide the salad leaves and half of the coriander leaves between 4 serving plates, and scatter over the grapefruit segments.

3 When ready to serve, drizzle the salad with the remaining dressing. Divide the crabmeat between the plates, spooning it neatly on top of the leaves. Scatter over the remaining coriander and serve immediately.

Rocket is a prolific and easy crop to grow. Here, its spicy leaves are combined with salty pancetta and Parmesan to make a quick pasta dish. Add the rocket only at the last minute.

Pasta with rocket
and pancetta

Serves 4 • **Prep** 5 mins • **Cooking** 15 mins

INGREDIENTS

1 tbsp extra virgin olive oil

1 onion, finely chopped

1 red chilli, deseeded and
    finely chopped

250g (9oz) pancetta, cubed

2 garlic cloves, grated or
    finely chopped

350g (12oz) spaghetti

200g (7oz) wild rocket leaves

sea salt and freshly ground
    black pepper

Parmesan cheese,
    grated, to serve

METHOD

1 Heat the oil in a large frying pan, add the onion, and cook over low heat for 5 minutes, or until soft and translucent.

2 Add the chilli and cook for a few minutes more. Add the pancetta and cook for 5 minutes, or until crisp and golden, then stir in the garlic, and cook for a few more seconds.

3 Meanwhile, cook the pasta in a large pan of boiling, salted water for 8–10 minutes, or until it is cooked but still has a bit of bite to it. Drain, keeping back a tiny amount of the cooking water.

4 Return the pasta to the pan and toss with the pancetta mixture. Add the rocket, season to taste with salt and pepper, and toss gently. Sprinkle with Parmesan and serve.

ROCKET

When to pick
Pick rocket leaves before they grow larger than 8–10cm (3–4in), as they can become very hot or bitter. Always pick leaves before the plant begins to bolt (run to seed).

Eat and store fresh
Young rocket can be washed, dried, and stored in a plastic bag in the fridge for up to 3 days.

How to preserve
Excess rocket can be made into rocket pesto (see page 55) and stored in the fridge for up to 1 week.

Rocket is one of the fastest growing salad crops. To keep on top of it, I like to make batches of this pesto to freeze. You can grow cultivated and wild types, but wild rocket can be bitter for cooking.

Rocket pesto

Makes approx. 200g (7oz) • **Prep** 10 mins • **Cooking** 2–3 mins

INGREDIENTS

50g (1³⁄₄oz) pine nuts

50g (1³⁄₄oz) rocket leaves, washed

10g (¹⁄₄oz) basil leaves (optional)

30g (1oz) Parmesan cheese, freshly grated

1 small garlic clove, crushed

sea salt and freshly ground black pepper

100ml (3¹⁄₂fl oz) extra virgin olive oil

METHOD

1 In a dry frying pan, over low heat, gently toast the pine nuts for 2–3 minutes, moving them all the time, until they are golden brown all over. Set aside to cool.

2 Put the rocket and basil leaves (if using), the cooled pine nuts, Parmesan, garlic, salt, and a good grinding of pepper into a food processor. Add 2–3 tbsp of the olive oil and process to a thick paste. If you are serving it with pasta, you can add a little more garlic and Parmesan, less if you are using it as an accompaniment to grilled chicken or fish.

3 With the motor running, continue to add the oil, in a thin stream, until the pesto becomes a thin paste. Try the pesto and adjust the seasoning, to taste. If you prefer a coarser texture, pulse in the food processor until you reach the desired consistency.

Note This will store in an airtight container for up to 5 days in the fridge and up to 2 weeks in the freezer.

RHUBARB

When to pick
Young, forced rhubarb can be picked early, the main crop picked when the stalks are still pink or red. After midsummer, leave the plant to rebuild its energy stocks.

Eat and store fresh
Although it may be eaten raw, rhubarb is usually cooked before eating. It will store in the fridge, washed and wrapped in newspaper, for up to 1 week.

How to preserve
Although low in pectin, rhubarb is delicious made into jam with fresh root ginger. It can also be used in chutneys, cordials, and syrups (see page 64).

Freezing options
Best frozen poached in syrup, or cooked and puréed (see pages 194–5).

In my allotment there is always an abundance of rhubarb in early summer. This ice cream, which gives a new twist to the traditional pairing of rhubarb and custard, is a lovely way of preserving it.

Rhubarb and custard
ice cream

Serves 4–6 • **Prep** 30 mins, plus chilling and freezing • **Cooking** 20 mins

INGREDIENTS

450g (1lb) pink forced rhubarb, cut into chunks
400g (14oz) caster sugar
5 egg yolks
pinch of salt
450ml (15fl oz) milk
150ml (5fl oz) single cream
1 tsp pure vanilla extract

METHOD

1 Gently stew the rhubarb with 60g (2oz) of the sugar and 2 tbsp water in a covered pan for about 10 minutes, or until really tender, stirring occasionally. Purée in a blender or food processor. Leave to cool.

2 Beat the egg yolks, remaining sugar, and salt in a large heatproof bowl with an electric beater or balloon whisk, until thick and pale. Gently heat the milk and cream until hand hot, and stir into the egg mixture with the vanilla. Put the bowl over a pan of gently simmering water and stir until the custard just coats the back of a wooden spoon. Remove the bowl from the pan and leave to cool.

3 When the custard is completely cold, mix with the rhubarb purée and freeze in an ice cream maker, following the manufacturer's directions. Alternatively, pour into a shallow, freezer-proof container with a lid, and freeze for about 2 hours until frozen around the edges. Beat well with a fork to break up the ice crystals, freeze for another 2 hours, beat again, then freeze until firm.

Note Store for up to 1 week in the freezer.

Rhubarb and ginger is a classic combination, the spicy warmth of ginger cutting through the sweet and sour flavour of rhubarb. Here, the rhubarb gives a new twist to a classic pavlova.

Rhubarb and ginger
meringue cake

Serves 4–6 • **Prep** 30 mins, plus cooling • **Cooking** 1 hour

INGREDIENTS

4 egg whites

pinch of salt

225g (8oz) caster sugar

For the filling

600g (1lb 5oz) rhubarb,
    cut into chunks

85g (3oz) caster sugar

4 pieces of stem
    ginger, chopped

$1/2$ tsp ground ginger

250ml (8fl oz) double cream

icing sugar, to dust

METHOD

1 Preheat the oven to 180°C (350°F/Gas 4). Place baking parchment on 2 baking trays.

2 Whisk the egg whites, salt, and 115g (4oz) of the sugar in a large, dry, glass or metal bowl. Whisk until stiff, glossy peaks form. Fold in the rest of the sugar, a spoonful at a time.

3 Divide the mixture between the baking trays and spread into two 18cm (7in) circles. Bake for 5 minutes, then reduce the oven temperature to 130°C (250°F/Gas $1/2$), and bake for 1 hour. Open the oven door and leave the meringues to cool completely.

4 Meanwhile, put the rhubarb, caster sugar, stem ginger, ground ginger, and 1 tbsp water in a large saucepan and cook, covered, over low heat for 20 minutes, or until soft. Allow to cool. Drain excess liquid, and chill until required.

5 Whip the cream and fold in the rhubarb. Place a meringue onto a serving plate, spread it with the rhubarb and ginger filling, then top with the remaining meringue. Dust with icing sugar and serve.

Preserving rhubarb as a purée ensures a ready supply for a quick dessert all year Fold into a combination of half whipped cream and half cold custard to make a delicious rhubarb fool.

Rhubarb and vanilla
freezer purée

Makes approx. 400g (14oz) • **Prep** 5 mins • **Cooking** 30 mins

INGREDIENTS

400g (14oz) rhubarb,
    cut into chunks
100g (3$^{1}/_{2}$ oz) granulated
    or light soft brown sugar
1 vanilla pod

METHOD

1 Place the rhubarb chunks in a saucepan. Add the sugar, 100ml (3$^{1}/_{2}$ fl oz) water, and the vanilla pod.

2 Bring the ingredients to a boil, then simmer for 25–30 minutes or until the rhubarb reduces. Stir occasionally to prevent the mixture from sticking to the base of the pan.

3 When the rhubarb is the consistency of a purée, take out the vanilla pod and put the purée into clean freezer pots, leaving 1cm ($^{1}/_{2}$ in) space at the top. Leave to cool, then seal and freeze.

This syrup has a heady, aromatic kick. Enjoy it diluted with water, or serve drizzled over ice cream. Pick your rose petals before they start to fade and use them quickly.

Rhubarb syrup
with rose petals

Makes approx. 500ml (16fl oz) or 2 small bottles • **Prep** 20 • **Cooking** 40–50 mins

INGREDIENTS

450g (1lb) pink or
    red-stemmed rhubarb,
    cut into short lengths
350g (12oz) granulated sugar
8 scented pink rose petals
2 tbsp rosewater
1 tsp citric acid

METHOD

1 Put enough water in a heavy saucepan to just cover the base. Add the rhubarb, sugar, and rose petals. Bring to a boil, stir gently, cover, reduce the heat, and cook for 20–30 minutes until really pulpy, stirring once or twice.

2 Strain the pulp in a jelly bag or a muslin-lined sieve set over a measuring jug or bowl. Press the pulp to extract maximum juice. Return the juice to the pan and bring back to a boil.

3 Remove from the heat and stir in the rosewater and citric acid. Pour immediately into warm, sterilized bottles using a sterilized funnel. Seal, label, and leave to cool, then store in the fridge. Shake before use.

Note The syrup will keep for 1 month, refrigerated.

SUMMER

French beans

Runner beans

Globe artichokes

Tomatoes

Peppers

Chilli peppers

Aubergines

Okra

Cucumbers

Courgettes

Sweetcorn

Fennel

Potatoes

Herbs

Gooseberries

Strawberries

Raspberries

Blackberries

Blueberries

Blackcurrants

Redcurrants

Melons

Cherries

Peaches

Apricots

FRENCH BEANS

When to pick
Harvest when
no more than
10–15cm (4–6in),
picking from the bottom
up and to encourage
regrowth. Leave some to
grow larger and use the
fresh beans inside.

**Eat and
store fresh**
Best eaten
as soon as they are
harvested, French beans
will keep for up to
3 days in the fridge. Eat
tiny beans raw in salads,
bigger ones cooked.

**How to
preserve**
Can be used as an
ingredient in pickles,
relishes, or chutneys.
The last of the beans
can be left on the plant
to dry and the pulses
harvested for winter use.

**Freezing
options**
Trim and slice, blanch
for 2–3 minutes, cool,
and freeze for up to
12 months.

French beans provide almost daily yields once they get into their stride. Here, some butter and a scattering of toasted hazelnuts turn them into an interesting side dish for most meats and fish.

French beans
with toasted hazelnuts

Serves 4 • **Prep** 5 mins • **Cooking** 5 mins

INGREDIENTS

250g (9oz) French beans,
    trimmed
sea salt
25g (scant 1oz) butter
75g (2½oz) hazelnuts, roughly
    chopped and toasted

METHOD

1 Put the beans in a pan of salted water and boil for 5–6 minutes, or until they are cooked but still have a bit of bite to them. Drain, then refresh under cold water so they stop cooking and retain their colour.

2 Transfer to a serving dish, top with the butter and toasted hazelnuts. These are particularly good served with roast chicken or lamb.

This delicious, Asian-inspired warm salad makes a great side dish for salmon or chicken, grilled with a teriyaki glaze. It works with any combination of French beans, sugarsnaps, or baby peas.

Warm French bean salad

Serves 6 • **Prep** 15 mins • **Cooking** 10 mins

INGREDIENTS

3 tbsp sesame seeds

450g (1lb) French beans,
    trimmed

250g (9oz) mangetout

3 shallots or spring onions,
    finely chopped

1 garlic clove, chopped

1 tbsp soy sauce

1/2 tbsp sesame oil

1/2 tbsp clear honey

2.5cm (1in) piece of
    root ginger, peeled
    and grated

sea salt and freshly ground
    black pepper

METHOD

1 Preheat the oven to 180°C (350°F/Gas 4). Place the sesame seeds on a roasting tray and roast for 8 minutes, or until the seeds are nicely browned; watch closely, as they burn easily.

2 Bring a large saucepan of salted water to a boil. Blanch the French beans for 3 minutes, then add the mangetout, and blanch for another minute.

3 Drain the beans and mangetout in a colander, and shake off any excess water. Combine all the remaining ingredients in a large serving bowl. Add the beans and mangetout, and toss to coat well. Sprinkle with the sesame seeds and serve.

This soup can be made using fresh or dried beans. Use fresh borlotti and haricot beans (found inside overgrown French beans) for an authentic take on this Mediterranean classic.

Soupe au pistou

Serves 6–8 • **Prep** 30 mins • **Cooking** 1¹/₂ hours

INGREDIENTS

3 garlic cloves

coarse sea salt

large handful of basil leaves

5 tomatoes, skinned, deseeded,
    and chopped

freshly ground black pepper

25g (scant 1oz) Mimolette
    cheese, grated

3 tbsp extra virgin olive oil

1 ham hock, about
    150g (5¹/₂ oz), or thick
    piece of bacon

200g (7oz) fresh white haricot
    beans, e.g. cannellini,
    shelled weight

100g (3¹/₂oz) fresh red haricot
    beans, e.g. borlotti,
    shelled weight

250g (9oz) flat green
    beans, sliced

2 medium floury potatoes, diced

4 medium courgettes, chopped

100g (3¹/₂ oz) small macaroni

METHOD

1 To make the pistou, pound the garlic in a large mortar with a pestle, then add a little salt and the basil, and pound to a paste. Add 2 of the tomatoes, and continue pounding and mixing until you have a thick sauce. Add pepper, cheese, and oil, mix well, and adjust the seasoning.

2 For the soup, put 2 litres (3¹/₂ pints) cold water in a large stewing pot. Add the ham hock. Bring to a simmer, then partly cover and leave to bubble gently for 30 minutes, skimming occasionally.

3 Meanwhile, put the haricot beans in a saucepan, cover with plenty of cold water, and bring to a boil. Simmer for 10 minutes, drain, and refresh. Add the rest of the vegetables with enough water to cover. Season lightly. Return to a simmer, then part-cover and bubble gently for 1 hour, skimming occasionally.

4 Remove the ham hock and shred the meat. Lift half of the ingredients out of the pan, mash with a fork, then return to the soup with the ham. Add the macaroni and cook until just tender. Stir in the pistou, and serve.

The red stripy pods of borlotti French beans are a beautiful sight. The cream and purple dappled beans inside are ideal for this slow-cooked dish, which tastes wonderful with grilled meats.

Borlotti beans
with tomatoes and capers

Serves 4–6 • **Prep** 10 mins • **Cooking** 1½ hours

INGREDIENTS

1 onion, finely chopped

2 garlic cloves, crushed

6 tbsp extra virgin olive oil

400g (14oz) can chopped
    tomatoes

100ml (3½fl oz) white wine

1 tsp caster sugar

sea salt and freshly ground
    black pepper

400g (14oz) borlotti beans,
    shelled weight

2 tbsp capers, rinsed, gently
    dried, and chopped

handful of basil leaves,
    finely chopped

1 tbsp balsamic vinegar

METHOD

1 In a large pan, cook the onion and garlic in 4 tbsp of the olive oil for 3 minutes or so, until softened, but not brown. Add the tomatoes, white wine, 100ml (3½fl oz) of water, sugar, and a good grinding of black pepper, and simmer, covered, for 20 minutes.

2 Mash up the sauce with a potato masher until the tomatoes are well crushed. Add the beans and another 100ml (3½fl oz) of water and simmer very gently, covered, for 45 minutes to 1 hour, until the beans are cooked through. You may need to add a little more water if the beans seem to be drying out.

3 Take the beans off the heat and add the capers, basil, balsamic vinegar, and the rest of the olive oil. Season to taste and serve warm or at room temperature.

Note If you do not grow borlotti beans and cannot find fresh beans to buy, you can make this recipe with 200g (7oz) of dried borlotti beans, soaked overnight and cooked according to packet instructions, before adding to the tomato and caper sauce.

Freeze vegetables

One of the best ways to preserve your home-grown vegetables is to freeze them. Most produce is best cooked before being frozen. Blanching vegetables, such as beans, before freezing them destroys the enzymes that cause their colour, texture, and flavour to deteriorate in the freezer. Other vegetables can be griddled or puréed, then frozen on open trays, before being packed into freezer bags, labelled, and dated. Frozen cooked and raw vegetables (except sweetcorn cobs) can be cooked from frozen, but cooked purées should be thawed before reheating.

1 **Blanch the beans** Bring a saucepan of lightly salted water to a boil. Add a handful of beans and bring back to a boil. Blanch each batch for 2–3 minutes.

2 **Cool the beans** Transfer each batch of beans immediately to a large bowl of iced water to halt the cooking process and set the colour. The beans will cool very quickly.

Freeze Blanched beans

Makes approx. 450g (1lb) • **Prep** 8 mins
Keeps 6–12 months in the freezer

INGREDIENTS

approx. 450g (1lb) French beans, trimmed

Other vegetables to freeze

The best vegetables to freeze are those with a firm, less watery texture:

Runner beans Slice, blanch, and open freeze.
Peas Wait for pods to swell before shelling, then blanch briefly and open freeze.
Spinach Blanch briefly and squeeze out moisture.
Sweetcorn Blanch and freeze whole cobs or first strip the kernels.
Tomatoes Cook and freeze batches of sauce.
Carrots Peel, slice, blanch, and open freeze, or cook first and freeze as a purée.

3 **Drain and dry** Remove the beans, drain, and pat them dry on kitchen paper. Leave to one side until all the batches have been blanched, drained, and dried.

4 **Pack and freeze** Pack in convenient portions in freezer bags or containers. Alternatively, freeze on open baking trays, then store in larger freezer bags.

RUNNER BEANS

When to pick
Best eaten when young, before they become tough and stringy. Pick runner beans when no more than 15cm (6in) long. Pick often to encourage regrowth.

Eat and store fresh
Before cooking, trim strings from the sides and slice diagonally into strips. Cook as soon as possible after harvesting. Store in the fridge for up to 3 days.

How to preserve
Use runner beans in pickles, relishes, and chutneys.

Freezing options
Trim, slice, and blanch for 2 minutes, cool, and freeze for up to 12 months.

Left to grow too large, runner beans have a tendency to become tough and stringy. It is often difficult to eat them as fast as they grow. This chutney is an ideal way to use up larger beans.

Runner bean
and courgette chutney

Makes approx. 1kg (2¼ lb) or 3 medium jars • **Prep** 30 mins • **Cooking** 2 hours

INGREDIENTS

600g (1lb 5oz) runner beans, thinly sliced

4 courgettes, thinly sliced

350g (12oz) cooking apples, peeled, cored, and chopped

2 onions, finely chopped

450g (1lb) light soft brown sugar

1 tsp mustard powder

1 tsp turmeric

1 tsp coriander seeds

600ml (1 pint) cider vinegar

METHOD

1 Put the beans, courgettes, apples, and onions in a preserving pan or a large, heavy, stainless steel saucepan. Then add the sugar, mustard powder, turmeric, and coriander seeds. Pour in the vinegar and stir.

2 Cook over gentle heat, stirring until all the sugar has dissolved, then bring to a boil and cook at a rolling boil, stirring occasionally, for about 10 minutes. Reduce to a simmer and cook for about 1½ hours, stirring from time to time, until the mixture thickens. Stir continuously near the end of cooking time so that the chutney doesn't catch on the base of the pan.

3 Ladle into warm, sterilized jars with non-metallic or vinegar-proof lids, making sure there are no air gaps. Cover each pot with a waxed paper disc, seal, and label. Store in a cool, dark place. Allow the flavours to mature for 1 month and refrigerate after opening.

Note The chutney will keep for 9 months unopened.

GLOBE ARTICHOKES

When to pick
The flower heads are best when harvested before the leaves open and flowers appear. Pick tight, firm heads from the centre of the plant to encourage regrowth.

Eat and store fresh
Best eaten immediately, the whole plant can be steamed or boiled or the heart can be eaten alone, after being steamed, boiled, or chargrilled.

How to preserve
Preserve cooked, whole baby globe artichokes in oil, or chargrill just the hearts before preserving them in oil (see page 81).

Freezing options
Trimmed hearts can be blanched for 4 minutes, cooled, and then frozen for up to 12 months.

This light, summer salad is a great way to use home-grown artichokes. You can either prepare raw artichokes, or take a short cut and use the baby artichokes preserved in oil (see opposite).

Artichoke salad

Serves 4 • **Prep** 25 mins, plus cooling • **Cooking** 10 mins

INGREDIENTS

4 globe artichokes

3 lemons

sea salt

2 large handfuls of rocket

25g (scant 1oz)
    Parmesan cheese

2 tbsp extra virgin olive oil

1 tbsp balsamic vinegar

freshly ground black pepper

METHOD

1 Trim the artichoke stalks and snap off the hard outside leaves (about 5–6 layers), until you reach the paler, more tender ones. Cut about 2.5cm (1in) off the spiny tips and discard. Then slice in half and using a teaspoon, carefully remove the choke and discard. Place the artichoke hearts in a bowl and pour the juice of 2 lemons over them.

2 Bring a saucepan of water to a boil. Add 1 tsp salt and the juice of the remaining lemon. Place the artichokes into the pan and cook for 10 minutes, or until tender. Drain well and set aside to cool.

3 When the hearts are cool enough to handle, carefully cut them into quarters.

4 Divide the rocket and artichokes between the serving plates. Using a vegetable peeler, shave pieces of Parmesan over each salad. Drizzle over with olive oil and balsamic vinegar, and season to taste with salt and pepper.

Baby artichokes are a great delicacy. They taste delicious when stored in olive oil. Serve as antipasti, or add to fresh pasta with home-made rocket pesto (see page 55).

Baby artichokes in oil

Makes approx. 500g (1lb 2oz) or 1 small jar • **Prep** 10 mins• **Cooking** 35 mins

INGREDIENTS

10 baby globe artichokes
300ml (10fl oz)
   white wine vinegar
1 tbsp sea salt

For the marinade
450ml (15fl oz) extra virgin
   olive oil
75ml (2$\frac{1}{2}$fl oz)
   white wine vinegar
handful of black peppercorns

METHOD

1 Trim the artichoke stalks and snap off the hard outside leaves (about 5–6 layers), until you reach the paler, more tender ones. Cut about 2.5cm (1in) off the spiny tips and discard. Then slice in half and using a teaspoon, carefully remove the choke and discard.

2 Put the vinegar, salt, and 300ml (10fl oz) of water in a preserving pan or heavy, stainless steel saucepan, and bring to a boil. Add the prepared artichokes and blanch for 3–5 minutes in the simmering vinegar mix. They should still retain plenty of bite. Drain, cool, then cut lengthways into quarters.

3 To prepare the marinade, put the olive oil, vinegar, and peppercorns into a saucepan and bring to a boil. Add the artichokes and bring back to the boil. Turn the heat off, and leave to cool with the artichokes in the marinade.

4 Using a slotted spoon, remove the cooled artichokes and put them into a sterilized jar with a non-metallic or vinegar-proof lid. Pour the marinade over to cover the artichokes. Seal, label, and store in the fridge. Once open, keep refrigerated, top up with oil if necessary so the artichokes are always covered, and use within 2 months.

TOMATOES

When to pick
Harvest tomatoes with deep colour and glossy skin. If signs of blight or disease show, pick any imperfect tomatoes immediately, to stop the disease spreading.

Eat and store fresh
Where possible, keep and eat tomatoes at room temperature for best flavour. Green tomatoes will keep for up to 2 weeks in a cool, dark place.

How to preserve
Tomatoes can be preserved in a number of ways, including in chutneys, sauces, or pickles. They can also be dried and preserved in oil (see pp.38–9 and 92–3).

Freezing options
Tomatoes freeze well if they have been cooked first. Typically, they are skinned, chopped, and cooked down before being cooled and frozen for up to 6 months.

This is a luxury version of a classic tomato soup. Fresh, roasted, and sun-dried tomatoes are combined to give a richness and depth of flavour to the finished dish.

Cream of tomato soup

Serves 4–6 • Prep 30 mins • Cooking 40 mins

INGREDIENTS

50g (1¾oz) butter

1 tbsp extra virgin olive oil

2 onions, finely chopped

2 celery sticks, finely chopped

2 carrots, finely diced

2 garlic cloves, crushed

12 plum tomatoes, about 1kg (2¼lb), quartered, roasted, and roughly chopped

8 plum tomatoes, about 600–720g (1¼–1½lb), skinned and finely chopped

6 sun-dried tomatoes, finely chopped

1 litre (1¾ pints) hot vegetable stock

2–3 tbsp double cream

sea salt and freshly ground black pepper

METHOD

1 Heat the butter and olive oil in a heavy saucepan over medium heat. Add the onions, and sauté for 8–10 minutes, stirring frequently, until very soft but not coloured. Next, add the celery and carrots, and continue cooking gently without burning for another 10 minutes, stirring from time to time. Add the garlic and sauté for another 2 minutes, stirring.

2 Mix together the roasted plum tomatoes, fresh tomatoes, and sun-dried tomatoes. Tip into the pan with any juices, and cook, stirring, for 5 minutes to allow the flavours to combine. If the sauce looks too thick or starts sticking to the bottom of the pan, add a little of the hot vegetable stock. Pour in the remaining vegetable stock, and simmer the soup for 15–20 minutes.

3 Blend the soup to a smooth purée using a food processor or hand-held blender. Pass through a sieve or mouli into a clean pan, unless you prefer to make a rougher textured soup. Add the double cream a teaspoon at a time until you are happy with the taste and texture. Season with salt and pepper, reheat very gently if required, and serve.

A time-honoured Spanish classic, this chilled tomato soup makes the best of high summer produce. It is delicious served simply with platters of sweet Charentais melon and salty Parma ham.

Gazpacho

Serves 6–8 • **Prep** 30 mins

INGREDIENTS

1 red pepper, deseeded
   and chopped

10 spring onions, trimmed and
   chopped, or 1 red onion,
   finely chopped

5 garlic cloves, chopped

1 cucumber, finely chopped

1kg (2¼lb) ripe tomatoes,
   finely chopped

1 tbsp thyme, marjoram,
   parsley, mint, or
   basil, chopped

100g (3½oz) stale bread

1 chilli, deseeded and finely
   chopped, or ½tsp cayenne
   pepper (optional)

2 tbsp red wine vinegar

3 tbsp extra virgin olive oil,
   plus extra to serve

sea salt and freshly ground
   black pepper

ice cubes

METHOD

1 Place a large serving bowl in the fridge. Put the pepper, spring onions or red onion, garlic, cucumber, and tomatoes in a mixing bowl, then add the herbs.

2 Whizz the bread in a blender to make breadcrumbs, then add to the mixing bowl along with the chilli or cayenne pepper (if using), the vinegar, and oil. Gradually add chilled water; 100ml (3½fl oz) will give it a nice thick consistency, but you can use more if you prefer.

3 Transfer to the blender and whizz briefly, until you achieve your preferred texture. Season generously with salt and pepper. Transfer to the serving bowl, add a few ice cubes, and drizzle with olive oil.

This Indian-style fish dish is quick to prepare and cook, making it ideal for entertaining. It can also be made using fillets of sea bass, John Dory, or any other firm, meaty fish.

Grilled red bream
with tomato and coriander salad

Serves 4 • **Prep** 15 mins • **Cooking** 6–8 mins

INGREDIENTS

4 red bream fillets, about
    150g (5½oz) each
lemon wedges, to serve

For the spice rub

3 tbsp walnut or extra
    virgin olive oil
4 tbsp chopped coriander
2 garlic cloves, crushed
1 tsp coriander seeds, crushed
1 tsp lemon juice
1 small green chilli,
    very finely chopped

For the tomato salad

4 plum tomatoes, chopped
1 tbsp chopped coriander
1½ tsp walnut or extra
    virgin olive oil
1 tbsp walnuts
sea salt and freshly ground
    black pepper

METHOD

1 Mix together all the ingredients for the spice rub and season with salt.

2 Line a baking sheet with foil and place the fish fillets on it, skin-side down. Brush the spice rub over the fish. Place under a hot grill for 6–8 minutes, until cooked through and lightly golden. Remove from the heat and keep warm.

3 Meanwhile, toast the walnuts in a dry frying pan, then lightly crush them, and mix with the rest of the ingredients for the tomato salad. Serve the fish with the salad and some lemon wedges.

If you grow a variety of different tomatoes, this salad is perfect for the best of the high summer crop as any type and combination of tomatoes can be used. The freshness of the ingredients is key.

Tomato salad
with mozzarella

Serves 4 • **Prep** 10 mins

INGREDIENTS

8 ripe plum tomatoes, sliced
6 cherry tomatoes, halved
1 small red onion, sliced
handful of basil leaves, torn
extra virgin olive oil,
    for drizzling
sea salt and freshly ground
    black pepper
2 handfuls of rocket leaves
balsamic vinegar, for drizzling
2 balls of mozzarella
    cheese, torn

METHOD

1 Put the tomatoes, red onion, and half the basil leaves in a bowl. Drizzle over plenty of olive oil, season well with salt and black pepper, and toss through.

2 Arrange the rocket leaves on a serving platter, and drizzle over a little olive oil and some balsamic vinegar. Season with salt and pepper, and spoon over the tomato and basil mixture.

3 Add the torn mozzarella. Scatter over the remaining basil leaves, and drizzle again with a little olive oil and balsamic vinegar. Serve immediately.

Slightly heating this vinaigrette brings out its strong, heady aromas. It works best served over freshly grilled tuna or salmon steaks, but is also good as a dressing for a pasta or rice salad.

Warm tomato
and garlic vinaigrette

Serves 4–6 • **Prep** 10 mins • **Cooking** 10 mins

INGREDIENTS

3 ripe, medium to
    large tomatoes
45ml (1^1/$_2$fl oz) extra virgin
    olive oil
2 garlic cloves, crushed
^{1}/$_4$ tsp hot paprika
1 tbsp finely chopped basil
1 tbsp finely chopped
    flat-leaf parsley
1 tbsp sherry vinegar
sea salt and freshly ground
    black pepper

METHOD

1 Place the tomatoes in a bowl, cover them with boiling water, and leave for 1 minute. Peel when they are cool enough to handle. Halve them, and then scoop out and discard the seeds. Remove the tomato core, dice the flesh, and set aside.

2 Put the olive oil in a pan over very low heat, and add the garlic and paprika. Stir for 3–4 minutes. Add half the basil and parsley, and stir for 1 minute. Add the tomatoes and stir gently for 2–3 minutes until hot.

3 Take off the heat. Stir in the reserved basil and parsley, and then the sherry vinegar. Season with salt and pepper to taste and serve while still warm.

Using the ripest tomatoes and the best olive oil, this dish captures the flavours of the Mediterranean. Serve it with freshly baked bread and a green salad for an elegant yet simple meal.

Baked ricotta
with roasted tomatoes

Serves 4 as a starter • **Prep** 15 mins • **Cooking** 25 mins

INGREDIENTS

2 tbsp extra virgin olive oil,
  plus extra for greasing
7 ripe cherry tomatoes,
  cut in half
sea salt and freshly ground
  black pepper
1 large red pepper
250g (9oz) ricotta
  cheese, drained
15g (1/2oz) Parmesan
  cheese, grated

METHOD

1 Preheat the oven to 220°C (425°F/Gas 7) and lightly grease a small roasting tin or dish. Reserve 2 tomato halves and place the rest in the tin, cut-sides up, then drizzle with 2 tbsp olive oil, and sprinkle with salt and pepper. Bake the tomatoes for 7–10 minutes or until they soften. Remove from the oven and set aside.

2 Place the pepper under a hot grill turning frequently for 4–5 minutes, or until blackened. Put the pepper in a plastic bag and set aside to cool, then peel. Cut in half, discard the core and seeds, and cut into strips. Set aside.

3 Cut the ricotta in half horizontally. Remove the tomatoes from the tin. Place the bottom half of the ricotta, cut-side up, in the tin and season lightly. Arrange the pepper strips on top, then the tomatoes. Drizzle with olive oil and top with the remaining ricotta, cut-side down.

4 Sprinkle with the Parmesan and drizzle with a little olive oil. Return to the oven and bake for 15 minutes, or until the cheese is hot and the crust is golden. Top with the reserved tomato halves and season with pepper.

This wonderful jam is extremely versatile, delicious served with cold meats, sausages, and cheese. It's ideal for the end of the tomato season, when there tends to be a late glut.

Tomato and chilli jam

Makes 350g (12oz) or 1 medium jar • **Prep** 10 mins • **Cooking** 35 mins

INGREDIENTS

500g (1lb 2oz) tomatoes
1 tsp chilli flakes
1 tsp dried, mixed herbs
juice of 1 lemon
pinch of salt
250g (9oz) granulated sugar

METHOD

1 Place the tomatoes in a bowl, cover them with boiling water, and leave for 1 minute. Peel when they are cool enough to handle. Halve them and then scoop out and discard the seeds. Remove the tomato core, roughly chop the flesh, and set aside.

2 Put all the ingredients, except the sugar, into a preserving pan or a large, heavy saucepan. Bring to a boil and simmer gently for about 8 minutes, or until the tomatoes break down and soften.

3 Add the sugar and heat gently, stirring until the sugar has dissolved. Turn up the heat and bring to a boil. When the jam reaches a rolling boil, cook for 10–15 minutes or until it starts to thicken and becomes glossy, reaching the setting point. Stir occasionally to prevent the jam sticking or burning in the pan. Remove the pan from the heat while you test for a set (see page 187).

4 Ladle into a warm, sterilized jar, cover with waxed paper, seal, and label. Store in a cool, dark place and refrigerate after opening.

Note The jam will keep for 6 months unopened.

By the end of the summer you may be left with lots of slightly imperfect tomatoes from your allotment. Chutneys and relishes are an ideal way to use up every last bit of your precious crop.

Tomato chutney
with roasted peppers

Makes approx. 1.35kg (3lb) or 3 medium jars • **Prep** 20 mins • **Cooking** 2 hours

INGREDIENTS

1 red pepper

1 orange pepper

1 yellow pepper

1.35kg (3lb) ripe tomatoes, plunged into boiling water for 1 minute, then skinned

2 onions, roughly chopped

450g (1lb) granulated sugar

600ml (1 pint) white wine vinegar

METHOD

1 Preheat the oven to 200°C (400°F/Gas 6). Put the peppers in a roasting tin and cook in the oven for 25–30 minutes until they begin to char. Remove from the oven, put in a plastic bag, and leave to cool before removing the stalks and skin, deseeding, and roughly chopping.

2 Put the tomatoes, peppers, and onions in a food processor and pulse briefly until chopped, but not mushy.

3 Tip the mixture into a preserving pan, or large, heavy, stainless steel saucepan, with the sugar and vinegar. Cook on low heat, stirring continuously, until the sugar has dissolved. Bring to a boil, reduce to a simmer, and cook for 1–1^1/$_2$ hours, stirring occasionally, until the mixture starts to thicken and turn jammy.

4 Ladle into warm sterilized jars with non-metallic or vinegar-proof lids, making sure there are no air gaps. Cover each pot with a waxed paper disc, seal, and label.

Note Store in a cool, dark place. Leave to mature for 1 month, and keeps for up to 9 months unopened.

Dry vegetables

Many fruits and vegetables are suitable to dry. If
you use top-quality produce, picked at its moment
of perfection, and dry it correctly, it will taste superb.
In warm countries, tomatoes are dried outside in the
sun for up to 4 days. Similar results can be achieved by
drying them in an oven on very low heat. Other fruits and
vegetables that dry well this way include mushrooms,
borlotti beans, sweetcorn, figs, pears, peaches, apricots, apples, and citrus peel.
Chillies and beans can be successfully air-dried (see right) for later use in recipes.

1 **Cut and score** Slice each tomato in half,
round ones horizontally, plum ones vertically.
Score the middle of each tomato half with a
cross shape and push the centres up from below.

2 **Sprinkle with salt** Arrange the tomato
halves cut side up, on wire racks over
baking trays. Sprinkle lightly with salt.
Leave for a few minutes. Place cut side down.

Recipe Oven-dried tomatoes

Makes approx. 900g (2lb) • **Prep** 10 mins, plus
8–12 hours drying, and cooling • **Keeps** 2 weeks,
refrigerated (12 months frozen)

INGREDIENTS

3kg (6½lb) ripe, but firm,
    medium-sized tomatoes

2–3 tsp sea salt

Air-drying beans and chillies

Beans that you can shell, such as borlotti and
climbing French beans (kidney beans), and red
chillies can be dried and stored at home.

Beans Dry the bean pods on newspaper then
shell the beans, arrange in trays, and place on a
window sill until dry and plump, but not wrinkled.
Keep in storage jars, out of direct sunlight, for
up to 1 year. Soak overnight before cooking.

Chillies Harvest red chillies and hang in
garlands to air-dry in a warm, dry, airy place
for 2 weeks. Use crumbled in recipes.

3 **Dry in the oven** Preheat the oven to
60–80°C/150–175°F/Gas ¼–½ and dry
for 8–12 hours, keeping the door slightly
ajar. Remove and leave to cool on the racks.

4 **Store in jars** Pack into sterilized jars and
store in the fridge. For long-term storage,
freeze on open trays, pack into bags, and
freeze. Thaw, cover with olive oil, and refrigerate.

PEPPERS

When to pick
You can harvest peppers when they are under-ripe (green), nearly ripe (yellow), or ripe (red). Generally the riper the pepper the sweeter the taste.

Eat and store fresh
Raw red peppers taste their best if eaten immediately, but all types of peppers will store well in the bottom of the fridge for up to 5 days.

How to preserve
Chutneys, pickles, and relishes are all good ways of preserving peppers. Chargrilling or roasting them, peeling, and preserving in oil is another option.

Freezing options
Peppers can be frozen if they are first griddled, then cooled, and stored in batches for up to 6 months. They also make good freezer pickles.

The chickpeas in this soup add depth and texture, making it a meal in itself. You can roast peppers ahead of time and keep them loosely packed in olive oil in the fridge for up to a week.

Roasted red pepper
and chickpea soup

Serves 4 • Prep 25 mins • Cooking 35 mins

INGREDIENTS

3 red peppers

1 Spanish onion, chopped

2 carrots, chopped

1 large garlic clove, chopped

2 tbsp chopped thyme

400g can chickpeas, drained

3 tbsp extra virgin olive oil,
    plus extra to garnish

1 tsp ground cumin

1 tsp ground cinnamon

2 tsp paprika

$^1/_2$ tsp grated root ginger

750ml (1$^1/_4$ pints) chicken
    or vegetable stock

1 tbsp tahini paste

1 tsp clear honey

sea salt and freshly ground
    black pepper

2 tbsp black olives, pitted

METHOD

1 Preheat the oven to 200°C (400°F/Gas 6). Put the peppers in a roasting tin and cook for 25–30 minutes until they begin to char. Remove from the oven, put in a plastic bag, and leave to cool before removing the stalks and skin, deseeding, and roughly chopping.

2 Heat the oil in a large pan and cook the onion, carrots, and garlic, over medium heat, stirring for 2 minutes until softened. Add the peppers, half the thyme, and all the remaining ingredients, except the olives. Bring to a boil, then reduce the heat, part-cover, and simmer gently for 30 minutes.

3 Purée using a hand-held blender or by transferring to a food processor, then reheat. Season to taste. Ladle into warm bowls, add a trickle of olive oil, and a sprinkling of chopped olives and thyme to each.

Note To save time, add raw, diced peppers in step 2. It is quicker, although the flavour is not as good.

In this Spanish dish, sweet red peppers are gently stewed, and then served cold. Wonderful as tapas or as a side dish with a piece of grilled steak or meaty fish, such as tuna.

Red pepper salad

Serves 4 • **Prep** 10 mins • **Cooking** 25 mins

INGREDIENTS

3 tbsp extra virgin olive oil

6 red peppers, deseeded and
    cut into large strips

2 garlic cloves, finely chopped

250g (9oz) ripe tomatoes,
    plunged into boiling water
    for 1 minute, then skinned,
    deseeded, and chopped

2 tbsp chopped parsley

sea salt and freshly ground
    black pepper

1 tbsp sherry vinegar

METHOD

1 Heat the oil in a large frying pan, add the peppers and garlic, and fry over low heat for 5 minutes, stirring, then add the tomatoes. Increase the heat, bring to simmering point, then reduce the heat to low, cover, and cook for 12–15 minutes.

2 Stir in the parsley, season well with salt and pepper, and cook for a further 2 minutes. Using a slotted spoon, remove the peppers, and arrange in a serving dish.

3 Add the vinegar to the pan, increase the heat, and simmer the sauce for 5–7 minutes, or until it has reduced and thickened. Pour the sauce over the peppers and allow to cool before serving.

Variation To make a red pepper dressing, process the salad in a blender or food processor until smooth. Whisk in enough olive oil to make a dressing, and use to coat a mix of green leaves.

This savoury scrambled egg dish is a classic recipe from the Basque region of southwest France, where the peppers have been sweetened by long hours of sunshine.

Pipérade

Serves 4 • **Prep** 5 mins • **Cooking** 20 mins

INGREDIENTS

2 tbsp extra virgin olive oil

1 large onion, finely sliced
   or chopped

2 garlic cloves, crushed

1 red pepper, deseeded
   and chopped

1 green pepper, deseeded
   and chopped

85g (3oz) Serrano ham or
   Bayonne ham, chopped

4 tomatoes, chopped

8 eggs, beaten

salt and freshly ground
   black pepper

2 tbsp chopped parsley,
   to garnish

METHOD

1 Heat the oil in a large frying pan and fry the onion over gentle heat until softened. Add the garlic and peppers, and fry for 5 minutes, stirring occasionally.

2 Add the ham and cook for 2 minutes, then add the tomatoes and simmer for 2–3 minutes, or until any liquid has evaporated.

3 Pour the eggs into the pan and scramble, stirring frequently. Season to taste with salt and pepper, sprinkle with parsley, and serve.

A wonderfully spicy vegetarian dish, where the contrasting lime and chilli work brilliantly well with the crunchy peanuts. Make it your own by adding the vegetables you have in season.

Fiery pepper noodles

Serves 4 • **Prep** 30 mins • **Cooking** 4–5 mins

INGREDIENTS

1 red pepper

1 green pepper

1 tbsp sunflower oil

4 spring onions, chopped

1 garlic clove, finely chopped

1 courgette, finely chopped

1 or 2 green jalapeño or
    poblano chillies, deseeded
    and chopped

1 tsp grated root ginger

1 tbsp chopped flat-leaf parsley

1 tbsp chopped coriander, plus
    a few torn leaves, to serve

grated zest and juice of 1 lime

4 tbsp crunchy peanut butter

3 tbsp soy sauce

1 tbsp dry sherry

9 tbsp water

500g (1lb 2oz) fresh
    egg noodles

60g (2oz) chopped roasted
    peanuts, to serve

METHOD

1 Preheat the oven to 200°C (400°F/Gas 6). Put the peppers in a roasting tin and cook for 25–30 minutes until they begin to char. Remove from the oven, put in a plastic bag, and leave to cool before removing the stalks and skin, deseeding, and roughly chopping.

2 Heat the oil in a wok or large frying pan. Add the spring onions, garlic, and courgette, and stir-fry for 1 minute. Add the peppers, chillies, ginger, herbs, lime zest and juice, peanut butter, soy sauce, sherry, and water. Stir until the peanut butter melts.

3 Add the noodles and toss for 2 minutes until piping hot. Pile into warm bowls and sprinkle with peanuts and a few torn coriander leaves.

For a small plant, the chilli can yield a surprising amount. A thin disc of chilli butter adds a touch of spice to grilled meats or fish, and can be frozen for convenient slicing whenever you need it.

Chilli butter

Makes 250g (9oz) • **Prep** 10 mins, plus chilling

INGREDIENTS

250g (9oz) butter, at room
    temperature
2 tbsp crumbled dried chillies
2 tsp ground cumin
2 garlic cloves, crushed
4 tbsp finely chopped
    coriander or parsley
sea salt and freshly ground
    black pepper

METHOD

1 Place the butter, chilli, cumin, garlic, and herbs in a mixing bowl and beat together until well combined. Season to taste with salt and pepper and stir again. Transfer to a sheet of greaseproof paper and mould it into a roll.

2 Wrap the roll with the paper and twist the ends to seal. Chill in the refrigerator for 1 hour, or until firm enough to slice.

Note The chilli butter can be made up to 3 days in advance and chilled until ready to use. Leftovers can be kept, wrapped in greaseproof paper, in the refrigerator, then sliced and melted for a quick butter sauce.

CHILLI PEPPERS

When to pick
You can harvest chillies at any stage of their ripeness. Their colour is an indicator of spiciness, so the darker and riper the chilli, the hotter the taste will be.

Eat and store fresh
Store fresh chillies in the fridge for up to 5 days. If left in a bowl in the kitchen, chillies can be used at any stage, as they will gradually start to dry.

 How to preserve
Dry chillies by tying together with string, and hanging them in a sunny window. Use in chutneys, relishes, butters, and chilli jelly (see page 102).

 Freezing options
Chillies can be frozen if made into chilli butter (see left).

CUCUMBERS

When to pick
Pick when small, to use whole or pickled, or grow longer for use in salads. Cucumbers should have a dark green, firm, glossy skin. Pick frequently to encourage regrowth.

Eat and store fresh
Eat small cucumbers soon after picking. Larger ones can be watery or bitter, so deseed and peel before use. Keep in the fridge for up to 5 days.

How to preserve
Cucumbers can be pickled, used in relishes, or salted for storage.

Freezing options
Cucumbers can be stored in the freezer as a freezer pickle (see pages 114–15).

This beautifully simple Scandinavian dish is an elegant accompaniment to a piece of grilled or cold poached salmon. The cooling cucumber adds colour as well as crunch.

Marinated cucumber
and dill salad

Serves 4–6 • **Prep** 10 mins, plus standing

INGREDIENTS

2 cucumbers, thinly sliced
    using a mandolin or
    food processor
2 tbsp coarse sea salt
2 tbsp caster sugar
4 tbsp rice wine vinegar,
    or white wine vinegar
freshly ground black pepper
handful of dill, finely chopped
juice of $1/2$ lemon (optional)

METHOD

1 Put the sliced cucumber in a colander and toss in the sea salt. Place a slightly smaller bowl on top of the cucumber and weigh down with weights, or a few unopened cans of food. Leave over a sink for 1 hour to allow the cucumber to lose any excess water.

2 Remove the weighted bowl, wrap the cucumber carefully in a clean tea towel and squeeze out the excess water. Transfer to a bowl, cover, and leave in the fridge for at least 1 hour, until completely chilled.

3 Meanwhile, put 2 tablespoons of boiling water into a bowl and stir in the sugar to dissolve. Then add the vinegar, a generous grinding of pepper, and the dill, and place the bowl in the fridge to cool. Once the dressing and cucumber are completely cold, mix the two together. Adjust the seasoning to taste before serving. If using rice wine vinegar, add the lemon juice.

The classic Vietnamese flavours of lime, chilli, and mint combine here to produce a wonderful summer salad. Be sure to get hold of some fish sauce, as it is vital to the taste of the finished dish.

Vietnamese salad
with cucumber and prawns

Serves 4 • **Prep** 15 mins • **Cooking** 2–3 mins

INGREDIENTS

12 large raw prawns

2 tbsp vegetable oil

1 tsp rice wine vinegar

1 tsp caster sugar

1 red chilli, deseeded and
   very finely chopped

2 garlic cloves, crushed

2 tbsp Vietnamese fish
   sauce or Thai fish sauce

1 tbsp lime juice

1 tbsp chopped rau ram
   (Vietnamese mint)
   or mint leaves, plus a few
   sprigs to serve

1 green papaya, deseeded,
   quartered lengthways,
   and thinly sliced

½ cucumber, deseeded
   and cut into thin strips

METHOD

1 Peel and devein the prawns, removing and discarding the heads and tails. Spread them out on a foil-lined grill rack, brush with the oil, and grill under medium heat for 2–3 minutes, or until they turn pink.

2 Meanwhile, whisk the rice wine vinegar, sugar, chilli, garlic, fish sauce, lime juice, and 75ml (2½fl oz) cold water together in a bowl until the sugar dissolves. Add the cooked prawns to the bowl and stir well until they are coated in the dressing. Leave to cool completely.

3 Add the chopped mint, papaya, and cucumber, and toss together. Transfer the salad to a serving platter, with the prawns on the top, and garnish with mint sprigs.

Here the aniseed flavour of tarragon combines beautifully with cream to produce an unusual, delicate side dish. Serve as an accompaniment to a piece of grilled salmon or chicken.

Cucumber
with tarragon cream

Serves 4 as a starter • **Prep** 15 mins, plus standing and finishing

INGREDIENTS

1 large, firm, unblemished
   cucumber, peeled
   and thinly sliced
2 tbsp coarse sea salt
$^1/_2$ tsp caster sugar
1 tbsp chopped tarragon,
   plus 2 tsp to finish
4 tbsp single cream, or
   3 tbsp soured cream
freshly ground black pepper

METHOD

1 Put the cucumber in a colander. Mix the salt, sugar, and tarragon, and sprinkle over the cucumber. Toss, then put a weighted plate on top. Leave for 30 minutes.

2 Rinse in plenty of cold water to get rid of any excess salt, drain well, and press down hard to extract all the moisture. Pat dry with kitchen paper.

3 Transfer to a serving bowl. Spoon over the cream, toss gently, and scatter over the reserved tarragon. Stir lightly, season with pepper, and serve.

Note This dish can be refrigerated overnight.

Make freezer pickles

Freezer pickles are a quick, modern way to achieve wonderfully fresh-flavoured condiments with bite and are a great way to preserve the best of your allotment vegetables. This cucumber pickle, which is so popular in sandwiches, can also be served with salads, cold meats, cheese, or barbecued fish. As with all frozen produce, only freeze fresh, top-quality food and freeze as quickly as possible for the best results.

1 **Draw out moisture** Thinly slice and chop the vegetables. Put into a large bowl, sprinkle the salt over them, mix well, and leave for 2 hours to draw out the moisture.

2 **Drain water** Tip the vegetables into a colander, rinse in cold water, and drain, pressing down lightly to squeeze out the moisture. Then put them into a clean, dry bowl.

Recipe Cucumber pickle

Makes 350–450g (12oz–1lb) • **Prep** 15 mins, plus standing • **Keeps** 6 months

INGREDIENTS

2 large cucumbers

2 shallots

1/2 green pepper (optional)

1–2 tsp sea salt

120ml (4fl oz) cider
   or wine vinegar

30–60g (1–2oz) caster sugar

pinch of ground turmeric
and celery seeds or dill
seeds, or 1/2–1 tsp
wholegrain mustard seeds

Other freezer pickles to try

Once you have learnt the principles of making freezer pickles, experiment with other vegetables, using what is available from your allotment.

Runner beans are ideal for a sweet-and-sour treatment with brown sugar and soy sauce. Leave the beans sprinkled in salt for 3 hours to draw out the excess moisture.

Cauliflowers work with cucumbers, red peppers, and spring onions to make a crunchy pickle. Sprinkle with salt and leave to stand for 3 hours.

3 **Soak in preserve** Mix the vinegar and sugar to taste. Stir to dissolve the sugar, then add the spices. Pour over the vegetables, cover, and refrigerate overnight.

4 **Transfer to pots** Store in freezer pots, leaving space at the top, seal, label, and freeze. To use, thaw overnight in the fridge, keep refrigerated, and use within 1 week.

Make cold pickles

Cold pickling is a simple but worthwhile process that can be used to make a variety of delicious condiments to last you throughout the year. With cold pickling, vegetables are salted to draw out moisture then stored in cold vinegar. For crisp pickles avoid diluted vinegar. Keep the vegetables submerged in their liquor and make sure that the metal lids of storage jars are not in direct contact with the pickle when storing, as the vinegar in the pickle will react with metal. Lids with plastic-coated linings are suitable for this purpose.

1 **Cut into quarters** Snip the stalk and any blossom from the cucumbers. You can leave the cucumbers whole, cut them into quarters lengthways, or into 3mm (1/8in) slices.

2 **Salt the cucumbers** In a bowl, layer the salt and cucumbers, finishing with a layer of salt. Leave at room temperature for 24 hours. Wash the cucumbers to remove the salt.

Recipe Pickled gherkins

Makes approx. 1kg (2¼lb) or 2 small preserving jars
Prep 20 mins, plus salting • **Keeps** 6 months

INGREDIENTS

500g (1lb 2oz) small
  pickling cucumbers,
  5–6cm (2–2½in) long,
  washed and rubbed dry
125g (4½oz) sea salt
3 or 4 shallots, peeled
1 or 2 garlic cloves, peeled

2–3 dried chillies (optional)
2–3 cloves (optional)
½ tsp dill seeds
2 sprigs of tarragon or dill
1 washed vine leaf (optional)
approx. 750ml (1¼ pints)
  white wine vinegar

Other cold pickles to try

The basic recipe for pickling shown here can
be adapted with many other vegetables:

Cabbages Pick firm small or medium-sized
heads, for a colourful, crisp pickle.
Cucumbers Cook in hot vinegar for a soft pickle.
Mixed vegetables Combine cauliflowers,
onions, carrots, tomatoes, and peppers for
a cold pickle.
Sweet shallots Lightly caramelize in balsamic
vinegar (see page 243).

3 Store in sterilized jars Pack into clean,
sterilized jars, leaving 1cm (½in) of head
space. Add the rest of the ingredients and
enough vinegar to cover the cucumbers.

4 Seal and store Seal the jars with
non-metallic or vinegar-proof lids and
label. Store in a cool, dark place for at
least 3–4 weeks to mature before eating.

COURGETTES

When to pick
Pick when no bigger than 15–20cm (6–8in) long, and before they become large, watery, and tasteless. Frequent picking encourages regrowth.

Eat and store fresh
Eat small courgettes raw in salads as soon as possible after picking. Keep larger ones in the fridge for 3–5 days.

How to preserve
Courgettes can be used in chutneys, pickles, and relishes, and can also be chargrilled and preserved in oil.

Freezing options
Slice smaller courgettes and blanch for 1 minute, leave to cool, and freeze for up to 6 months.

Lovely when picked young, this member of the concurbit family soon resembles the marrow if left to grow larger than your hand. To offset any wateriness, salt larger courgettes before use.

Courgette fritters
with dill tzatziki

Serves 4 (makes 12 small fritters) • **Prep** 20 mins, plus draining • **Cooking** 10 mins

INGREDIENTS

200g (7oz) courgettes, coarsely grated
sea salt and freshly ground black pepper
100g (3½oz) ricotta cheese
1 large egg
2 tbsp plain flour
3 garlic cloves, crushed
small handful of basil, chopped
small handful of flat-leaf parsley, chopped
light olive oil, to fry
2 tbsp finely chopped dill
200g (7oz) Greek-style yogurt
juice of ½ lemon

METHOD

1 Sprinkle the courgettes with 1 tsp of salt and leave to drain in a sieve for 1 hour. Rinse and squeeze dry in a clean tea towel.

2 In a bowl, whisk together the ricotta cheese, egg, and flour. Add 2 of the crushed garlic cloves, the basil, and parsley, and season well. Mix in the courgettes.

3 Fill a frying pan with olive oil to a depth of 1cm (½in) and fry tablespoons of the courgette batter over medium heat for 2–3 minutes on each side, until golden brown. Drain on kitchen paper.

4 To make the tzatziki, mix the last clove of garlic with the dill, some salt and pepper, and the yogurt. Add a squeeze of lemon juice and serve immediately with the hot fritters.

Anyone that grows them well knows that courgettes are prolific and can double in size almost overnight. You can use larger fruits here, as they are marinated and drained of excess water.

Courgettes
with chive marinade

Serves 4 as a starter • **Prep** 20 mins plus standing

INGREDIENTS

400g (14oz) courgettes

4 tbsp extra virgin olive oil

2 tbsp lemon juice, and 1 tbsp
    finely grated lemon zest

1 tsp finely chopped chives,
    plus 2 tsp to finish

1 tsp finely chopped flat-leaf
    or curly parsley, plus
    1 tsp to finish

1 tsp finely chopped thyme

sea salt and freshly ground
    black pepper

METHOD

1 Rinse the courgettes, pat them dry, and then top and tail them. Using a vegetable peeler, shave lengthways into thin strips (it doesn't matter if some strips are just peel or a little thicker); if using larger courgettes discard the central seeds. Reserve on a plate lined with a double layer of kitchen paper.

2 In a bowl, mix 1 tbsp of the olive oil with the lemon juice and zest, chives, parsley, and thyme, and season lightly with salt and pepper. Add the courgette strips and toss to coat. Leave to stand in a cool place for at least 40 minutes.

3 Tip into a colander. Drain well, pressing down gently, then pat dry with kitchen paper.

4 Transfer to a serving bowl. Spoon over the reserved olive oil, chives, and parsley, and toss lightly. Taste and season with salt and pepper. Serve at room temperature.

Pea shoots, the first tendrils of the young plants, can be enjoyed raw in salads and other dishes. Combine them with fresh baby peas and raw courgettes in this vibrant, healthy dish.

Courgette
and pea tortilla

Serves 10 as canapés • **Prep** 20 mins • **Cooking** 5 mins

INGREDIENTS

500g (1lb 2oz) courgettes,
   grated
50g (1³/₄oz) baby
   spinach leaves
grated zest and juice of 1 lemon
250g (9oz) baby peas
50g (1³/₄oz) toasted pine nuts
sea salt and freshly ground
   black pepper
10 wheat tortillas, halved
2 tbsp reduced-fat mayonnaise
large handful of mangetout
   (snow pea) sprouts and pea
   shoots

METHOD

1 In a large bowl, mix together the courgettes, spinach, lemon zest and juice, peas, and pine nuts. Season with salt and pepper.

2 Heat a dry frying pan over high heat. Add the tortilla halves, 2 at a time, and toast for about 15 seconds on each side. As you cook, set aside the tortilla halves under a clean tea towel to keep warm.

3 Lay one of the tortilla halves flat on a chopping board, and brush lightly with the mayonnaise. Take some of the courgette filling, and place in the centre. Arrange some of the mangetout sprouts and pea shoots on top, so that they stick out at one end, then gently roll up the mini tortilla. Repeat this process until you have made 20 tortillas.

4 To serve, arrange the mini tortillas on individual serving plates, allowing 2 per person.

The vibrant green of grated courgette combines with the creamy white of goat's cheese to make this beautiful omelette. Strewn with fresh thyme, the finished dish looks almost too good to eat.

Grated courgette
and goat's cheese omelette

Serves 1 • **Prep** 10 mins • **Cooking** 5 mins

INGREDIENTS

3 eggs, lightly beaten

1 small courgette, grated

sea salt and freshly ground
     black pepper

knob of butter

50g (1³/₄oz) soft goat's
     cheese, crumbled

small handful of thyme, leaves
     picked, to garnish (optional)

METHOD

1 Put the eggs and courgette in a jug. Season with salt and black pepper.

2 Melt the butter in a small non-stick frying pan over medium-high heat until foaming, then pour in the egg mixture, swirling it around the pan to cover the base. Gently slide a knife under the edges of the omelette.

3 When the omelette is beginning to cook around the edges, scatter over the goat's cheese, so that it is evenly covered. Continue cooking until the centre is almost cooked, but still just a little wet. Remove from the heat, and leave for 2 minutes to set; the retained heat will continue to cook the omelette.

4 Sprinkle over a little black pepper, and garnish with thyme leaves (if using). Carefully slide the omelette out of the pan and serve immediately.

SWEETCORN

When to pick
Pick sweetcorn when the silky tassels at the top of the plant are withering and brown. Ripe kernels should produce a milky white liquid when pressed.

Eat and store fresh
Eat sweetcorn as soon as possible after picking. If you must store it, keep the outer husk intact, and it will stay fresh for 2–3 days in the fridge.

How to preserve
Sweetcorn can be used in chutneys, pickles, and relishes (see pages 128–9).

Freezing options
Cut the sweetcorn off the cob with a sharp knife and blanch for 2 minutes, then cool and freeze for up to 12 months.

Home-grown sweetcorn is so tender that there is no need to cook it before making these fritters. The generous flavours used here will turn your cobs into something the whole family will enjoy.

Sweetcorn fritters
with tomato salsa

Serves 4 (makes 14–16 fritters) • **Prep** 20 mins • **Cooking** 10 mins

INGREDIENTS

2 sweetcorn cobs, around 250g (9oz)

100g (3½oz) self-raising flour

1 tsp baking powder

2 large eggs

4 tbsp milk

1 tsp smoked paprika

2 spring onions, finely chopped, green and white parts separated

4 tbsp chopped coriander

1 red chilli, deseeded and finely chopped (optional)

sea salt and freshly ground black pepper

2 tbsp sunflower oil

2 ripe tomatoes, skinned and roughly chopped

2 tbsp extra virgin olive oil

dash of Tabasco or chilli sauce

METHOD

1 Hold the corn upright on a chopping board and, using a sharp knife, cut downwards to shear off the kernels from the husk.

2 Sift the flour and baking powder into a bowl. Mix the eggs and milk together in a jug, and then gradually whisk them into the flour to make a thick batter. Add the corn, paprika, the white parts of the spring onions, 2 tbsp of the coriander, and the chilli (if using). Mix well and season.

3 Heat the sunflower oil in a large frying pan and add the batter mixture in tablespoonfuls. Use the back of the spoon to spread the fritters out slightly, and fry for 2–3 minutes on each side until puffed up and golden brown. Batch fry until all the mixture is cooked, adding a little more sunflower oil as necessary.

4 Put the tomatoes, the remaining coriander and spring onion, olive oil, and Tabasco or chilli sauce into a food processor or blender, and process until blended but still quite chunky. Check the salsa for seasoning and serve the hot fritters with the salsa on the side.

The sweetness of freshly harvested cobs cannot be beaten. We often cook sweetcorn on a stove at the allotment straight away, but if any makes it home, this is a wonderful soup to use it in.

Sweetcorn chowder

Serves 4–6 • **Prep** 10 mins • **Cooking** 30 mins

INGREDIENTS

4 sweetcorn cobs
500ml (16fl oz) water
sea salt
2 bay leaves
2 tbsp extra virgin olive oil
1 large onion, chopped
4 fresh sage leaves,
    chopped, or $\frac{1}{2}$ tsp
    dried sage, crushed
1 tsp fresh thyme leaves,
    or $\frac{1}{2}$ tsp dried thyme
1 medium carrot, chopped
2 celery sticks, chopped
1 large potato, chopped
200g (7oz) cream cheese
120ml (4fl oz) whole milk
freshly ground black pepper
single cream, to serve
dusting of paprika, to serve

METHOD

1 Stand each corn cob upright in a large bowl and strip the kernels by cutting downwards with a sharp knife. Set the kernels aside. Place the cobs in a large pan and add water, a generous dose of salt, and bay leaves. Bring to a boil and simmer, covered, for 15 minutes. Remove and discard the cobs and bay leaves, and reserve the liquid.

2 Heat the olive oil in a pan and cook the onions until translucent. Add the herbs and remaining vegetables, except the corn kernels. Cook for about 5 minutes, until softened. Add the corn cob stock and simmer until the potato is collapsing. Meanwhile, place the sweetcorn kernels in a pan and barely cover with cold water. Bring to a boil and cook for 2 minutes. Set aside.

3 Add the cream cheese and milk to the soup mixture, then purée until smooth using a hand-held blender or transferring to a food processer. Stir in the corn kernels with their cooking liquid. Give the chowder one more whizz, if desired, to break up the corn kernels slightly. Reheat and adjust the seasoning. Ladle into warm bowls. Drizzle with streaks of single cream and dust with paprika.

Make relish

Made from diced fruit or vegetables, relish is part-pickle, part-chutney, but cooked for a shorter time than a chutney. As its name implies, relish packs a tangy punch of flavour and is a classic accompaniment to barbecued food and burgers. Be sure to prepare all the ingredients meticulously as the final texture of your preserve is dependent on your care at this stage. Take the time to chop the ingredients finely, unless you prefer a chunkier relish. It is up to you what extra flavourings you add for spice. This recipe uses chilli, but you can leave this out if you prefer. Relishes can be eaten immediately or stored.

1 **Strip and blanch** Strip the kernels from the cobs using a sharp knife. Blanch the kernels in a saucepan of boiling water for 2 minutes, then drain well.

2 **Simmer in the pan** Put the sweetcorn and the other ingredients in a saucepan, bring to a boil, and stir. Simmer gently, stirring frequently, for 15–20 minutes.

Harvesting home-grown potatoes is so rewarding. If you have successfully grown your own potatoes, they deserve to be made into something as delicious as this spicy Spanish dish.

Patatas bravas

Serves 4 • **Prep** 15 mins • **Cooking** 1 hour

INGREDIENTS

6 tbsp extra virgin olive oil

700g (1lb 9oz) white potatoes, peeled and cut into 2cm (¾in) cubes

2 onions, finely chopped

1 tsp chilli flakes

2 tbsp dry sherry

zest of 1 lemon

4 garlic cloves, grated or finely chopped

½ x 400g can chopped tomatoes

handful of flat-leaf parsley, chopped

sea salt and freshly ground black pepper

METHOD

1 Preheat the oven to 200°C (400°F/Gas 6). Heat half the oil in a non-stick frying pan, add the potatoes, and cook, turning frequently, over medium-low heat for 20 minutes, or until starting to brown. Add the onions and cook for another 5 minutes.

2 Add the chilli, sherry, lemon zest, and garlic and allow to reduce for 2 minutes before adding the tomatoes and parsley. Season with salt and black pepper, combine well, and cook over medium heat for 10 minutes, stirring occasionally.

3 Add the remaining oil, place the whole lot in a shallow baking dish, and cook in the oven for 30 minutes. Serve hot with a selection of tapas dishes.

Note You can cook the potatoes on the hob instead, although oven-cooking intensifies the flavour.

A Spanish classic, this tortilla can be eaten warm or cold and makes perfect picnic food. Dice it into small squares and serve with olives and salted almonds before a meal, as the Spanish do.

Spanish tortilla

Serves 4 • **Prep** 10 mins • **Cooking** 45 mins

INGREDIENTS

300ml (10fl oz) extra virgin olive oil, plus 1 tbsp for frying

5 medium potatoes, peeled and sliced, about 5mm (¼in) thick

3 medium onions, quartered and sliced

sea salt and freshly ground black pepper

5 eggs

METHOD

1 Put the olive oil in a deep-sided ovenproof frying pan (preferably non-stick), add the potatoes, and cook at a gentle simmer for about 15 minutes, or until they are soft. Remove the potatoes with a slotted spoon and put them in a large bowl to cool.

2 Tip most of the oil out of the pan, add the onions and a pinch of salt. Cook over low heat until soft and beginning to caramelize. Add to the potatoes and leave to cool.

3 Whisk the eggs with a fork, then pour into the cooled potato and onion mixture, season with salt and pepper, and combine gently so all the potatoes get coated.

4 Preheat the oven to 200°C (400°F/Gas 6). Heat 1 tbsp of olive oil in the frying pan until hot, then carefully slide the egg mixture in, spreading it evenly so it covers the base of the pan. Reduce the heat to medium-low and cook for 6–10 minutes, or until almost set.

5 Put in the oven, and cook for a further 10 minutes, or until set and golden. Alternatively, cook one side, then invert onto a plate and add back to the pan to cook the other side. Remove from the pan, leave to cool and set, then slice into wedges. Serve warm or cold.

Going by the delightful name of "wrinkly potatoes", this dish originates in the Canary Islands. Serve as tapas with other dishes, or as a light lunch with a crisp green salad.

Papas arrugadas

Serves 4–6 as tapas • **Prep** 15 mins • **Cooking** 45 mins

INGREDIENTS

1kg (2¼lb) new potatoes, scrubbed

coarse sea salt and freshly ground black pepper

100ml (3½fl oz) extra virgin olive oil

1 red pepper

juice of 1 lemon

2 heaped tbsp tomato purée

1 tsp smoked paprika

½ tsp ground cumin

pinch of chilli powder, or to taste

1 garlic clove, crushed

2 tbsp chopped flat-leaf parsley or coriander (optional)

METHOD

1 Preheat the oven to 200°C (400°F/Gas 6). Place the potatoes on a baking tray, toss in salt and 1 tablespoon of the olive oil, and roast whole for about 45 minutes or until golden brown, turning occasionally.

2 Meanwhile, rub the pepper in olive oil and roast in the same oven for around 30 minutes, turning occasionally, until tender and soft. Remove the pepper from the oven, place it in a plastic bag for 2–3 minutes to loosen the skin, then cool, peel, and deseed. Roughly chop the cooked pepper.

3 Process the pepper, lemon, tomato purée, spices, and garlic, together with the remaining oil, in a food processor or using a hand-held blender to form a thick, unctuous dipping sauce. Add a little more oil if needed. Check the seasoning, add the parsley or coriander (if using), and serve with the potatoes.

Note If you have leftover sauce it can be stored in the freezer for 1 month.

A fantastically hearty supper dish, serve this twist on a classic Dauphinoise recipe with green beans or a salad. The emmental and pancetta lift the humble potato to a higher level.

Potatoes Dauphinoise
with emmental and pancetta

Serves 4–6 • **Prep** 20 mins • **Cooking** 45 mins

INGREDIENTS

200g (7oz) cubed pancetta

1.5kg (3lb 3oz) potatoes, peeled and thinly sliced

300ml (10fl oz) whole milk

300ml (10fl oz) double cream

150g (5½oz) emmental, sliced

sea salt and freshly ground black pepper

METHOD

1 In a frying pan, over medium heat, cook the pancetta until starting to crisp. Remove, and drain on kitchen paper.

2 Preheat the oven to 200°C (400°F/Gas 6). In a large pan, simmer the potatoes in the milk and cream for 10–15 minutes, then remove with a slotted spoon (reserve the milk and cream mixture).

3 Layer the potatoes in a large gratin dish with the emmental and pancetta, and season. Pour over the milk and cream, cover with foil, and cook in the oven for 45 minutes. Remove the foil for the last 15 minutes of cooking time to brown the top.

These delicious little cakes can be eaten simply on their own or as a side dish. Try them with some smoked salmon, a poached egg, and a spoon or two of hollandaise sauce.

Potato cakes
with Parmesan

Serves 4 • **Prep** 20 mins • **Cooking** 20 mins

INGREDIENTS

750g (1lb 10oz) floury potatoes, such as Maris Piper, peeled and cut into chunks

1 large egg yolk

50g (1³/₄oz) Parmesan cheese, finely grated

sea salt and freshly ground black pepper

30g (1oz) plain flour

sunflower oil or vegetable oil, for frying

1 tbsp capers, drained

1 lemon, cut into wedges

METHOD

1 Place the potatoes in a large pan of cold salted water, bring to a boil, and simmer for 15 minutes, or until tender. Drain well, then pass through a potato ricer or sieve, set over a bowl. Alternatively, mash well.

2 Add the egg yolk and Parmesan to the potato, season to taste with salt and pepper, and mix. Divide into 8 equal balls and flatten into little cakes, each 5cm (2in) in diameter. Tip the flour onto a plate, season with salt and pepper, then coat the potato cakes in the flour, and chill until needed.

3 Pour enough oil into a frying pan to cover the bottom and set it over medium heat. Fry the potato cakes in batches for 2 minutes on each side, or until golden and hot. Remove from the pan and drain on kitchen paper.

4 Increase the heat and fry the capers for 45 seconds, or until crisp. Drain on kitchen paper. Lift the cakes onto warm plates, scatter the capers, and serve with lemon wedges.

Store under soil

Clamping is a traditional way of storing potatoes and other root vegetables, if you haven't got a store room or a root cellar. Site a clamp in a sheltered spot as it is not guaranteed frost-protection and is not suitable in areas where frosts are severe or common. To prepare potatoes for clamping, carefully dig them up on a dry day, shake off the excess soil, and leave to dry outside for 1–2 hours to "set" the skins. Only use perfect specimens for clamping.

1 **Dry potatoes** Leave the potatoes to dry for 1–2 hours and dig a trench 10cm (4in) deep, 1m (3ft) in diameter, in a sheltered, well-drained site. Layer the trench with sand.

2 **Form a pyramid** Heap straw over the trench 20cm (8in) high, and arrange the potatoes in the centre in a pyramid shape. Leave them to breathe for 1–2 hours.

Clamp Potatoes

Keeps 4–5 months

YOU WILL NEED

potatoes, to form a pyramid no bigger
    than 50cm (20in) high

clean straw

sand

spade

soil

an area of sheltered, well-drained soil

3 Add straw Place a 10–20cm (4–8in) thick layer of straw over the top. Cover with a 15cm (6in) layer of soil. Leave a 5cm (2in) hole at the top and fill it loosely with straw.

4 Pack down the soil Pack the soil down around the sides of the clamp with the back of a spade. Dig a shallow drainage trench around the base of the clamp.

CORIANDER

When to pick
Pick coriander when it is young and before the leaves start to yellow or become too large. If growing for seeds, leave the flower heads to dry on the plant before harvesting.

Eat and store fresh
Keep coriander in a glass of water, in or out of the fridge, or wrapped in damp kitchen paper in the fridge for 2–3 days. Use fresh whenever possible.

How to preserve
Use coriander in a pesto and store in the fridge for up to 2 weeks. Alternatively, dry the leaves flat or hang them to dry for 2 weeks, then store in sealed glass jars for up to 6 months (see pages 160–1).

Freezing options
Freeze in a herb butter or by adding oil and putting into freezer bags, or by freezing in ice cubes (see pages 148–9).

Try this tasty alternative to the more usual basil and pine nut pesto. It can be used in the same way, with pasta or as a canapé spread on crostini, topped with a piece of soft goat's cheese.

Coriander
and walnut pesto

Makes approx. 175g (6oz) or 1 small jar • **Prep** 10 mins

INGREDIENTS

1 small bunch of coriander, approx. 30g (1oz), stalks removed
1 large garlic clove, lightly crushed
30g (1oz) walnut pieces
sea salt and freshly ground black pepper
30g (1oz) Parmesan cheese, grated
5 tbsp extra virgin olive oil

METHOD

1 Put the coriander leaves in a blender or food processor with the garlic, walnuts, a generous grinding of black pepper, a pinch of salt, cheese, and 1 tbsp of the oil. Blend the ingredients, stopping to scrape down the sides of the bowl as necessary.

2 With the machine still running, gradually add 3 tbsp of the remaining oil, a little at a time, until you have a glistening, thinnish paste. Alternatively, pound the coriander and garlic using a mortar and pestle. Gradually add the nuts, crushing them to a paste with the herbs. Add the pepper and salt, work in a little of the cheese, then a little of the oil, and continue until both are used up (reserving 1 tbsp of oil), and you have a glistening paste.

3 Spoon into a sterilized jar, top with the remaining 1 tbsp of oil to prevent air getting in, screw on the lid, and store in the fridge.

Note Keeps for 2 weeks, refrigerated. If you don't use all the pesto in one go, cover the remainder with another 1 tbsp of olive oil and screw the lid back on tightly.

BASIL

When to pick
Keep a pot of basil on your window sill and pick as required. If grown outdoors, pinch off the larger stems above a set of leaves, using larger leaves first.

Eat and store fresh
Store wrapped in damp kitchen paper in the fridge for up to 2 days. Use fresh whenever possible. Older basil can be chopped and added at the end of cooking to many recipes.

How to preserve
Use basil in a pesto and store in the fridge for up to 2 weeks. Alternatively, dry the leaves flat or hang them to dry for 2 weeks, then store in sealed glass jars for up to 6 months (see pages 160–1).

Basil works particularly well in this very adaptable recipe, but you can try other green herbs such as dill, sorrel, mint, or coriander to match whatever you are serving it with.

Herbed mayonnaise

Makes 450ml (15fl oz) • **Prep** 10 mins

INGREDIENTS

2 tbsp white wine vinegar

1 egg and 2 egg yolks

1 tbsp Dijon mustard

1 tbsp light soft brown sugar

1 garlic clove

sea salt and freshly ground
    black pepper

300ml (10fl oz) sunflower oil

30g (1oz) basil, or other
    green herbs

METHOD

1 Put the vinegar, egg, egg yolks, mustard, sugar, and garlic, in a food processor and add ¹/₂ tsp each of salt and pepper. With the motor running, slowly pour in the oil in a steady stream until the sauce is thick and creamy.

2 Transfer to a bowl and stir in the finely chopped herbs until they are thoroughly incorporated.

Note A squeeze of lemon or lime juice, or a dash of chilli, can also be added to the finished mayonnaise. This sauce may be made 2–3 days in advance, and chilled until ready to use.

The delicate flavours of this sophisticated, chilled custard work surprisingly well when paired with summer fruits such as strawberries, raspberries, or blackcurrants.

Basil and vanilla custard

Serves 4–6 • **Prep** 20 mins • **Cooking** 30 mins, plus cooling

INGREDIENTS

500ml (16fl oz) whole milk

3 tbsp basil leaves, plus a few
    small leaves to decorate

2 vanilla pods, split
    lengthways and deseeded

3 large or 4 medium
    egg yolks

6 tbsp caster sugar

1 tsp cornflour

3 tbsp crème fraîche

Szechuan pepper (optional),
    to garnish

METHOD

1 Put the milk in a pan. Squash the basil leaves and add to the milk. Add the vanilla pods and seeds and simmer over low heat, stirring occasionally. When the milk starts to bubble, reduce the heat to low, and cook gently, stirring frequently, for 10 minutes. Take off the heat and set aside.

2 In a large bowl, whisk together the egg yolks and sugar until smooth and pale. Whisk in the cornflour.

3 Use a fine sieve to strain the hot milk a little at a time into the egg yolk and sugar mixture. Push down the basil and vanilla into the sieve, then discard. Whisk the yolk mixture well between additions.

4 Return the mixture to the pan over very low heat. Bring to a gentle simmer, stirring constantly, for 10 minutes or until the custard has thickened enough to coat the back of a spoon. Do not allow it to boil. If necessary, take it off the heat from time to time.

5 Leave to cool, stirring occasionally. Stir in the crème fraîche, and when completely cold, place it in the fridge. Serve well chilled, decorated with small basil leaves and with a little Szechuan pepper on top (if using).

DILL

When to pick
Pick dill when the fronds are dark green and glossy. If you are growing it for the seeds, leave the flower heads to dry on the plant before harvesting.

Eat and store fresh
Keep dill in a glass of water, in or out of the fridge, or wrapped in damp kitchen paper in the fridge for 3 days. Use fresh where possible. Dill can be used in salads (see page 110), or with fish, or new potatoes.

How to preserve
Hang sprigs tied with string to dry for at least 2 weeks in a dry, airy room out of direct sunlight. Store in sealed glass jars for up to 6 months (see pages 160–1).

Freezing options
Freeze in a herb butter, or by adding oil and putting into freezer bags, or by freezing in ice cubes (see pages 148–9).

Fresh and citrus, this salsa makes a perfect partner for all types of fish and seafood. Its robust flavours are also well suited to grilled or barbecued meats.

Dill and tomato salsa
with watercress and capers

Serves 4–6 • **Prep** 15 mins, plus chilling

INGREDIENTS

2 tbsp chopped dill fronds

50g (1³/₄oz) picked watercress leaves, chopped

9 baby cherry tomatoes, halved

1 heaped tbsp capers, drained

juice and finely grated zest of ¹/₂ lemon

sea salt and freshly ground black pepper

3 tbsp extra virgin olive oil

METHOD

1 Put the dill and watercress in a bowl. Gently squeeze the halved cherry tomatoes to discard some of the seeds, then slice into quarters, and add to the bowl. Stir in the capers (if they are large, chop them first), and lemon juice and zest. Chill for 30 minutes or until ready to use.

2 Stir, season with salt and pepper, and drizzle with olive oil. Stir again before serving.

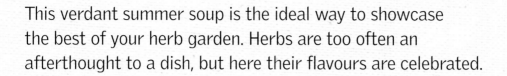

This verdant summer soup is the ideal way to showcase the best of your herb garden. Herbs are too often an afterthought to a dish, but here their flavours are celebrated.

Cream of herb soup

Serves 4–6 • **Prep** 15 mins • **Cooking** 1 hour

INGREDIENTS

2 tbsp butter

30g (1oz) each, chopped onion and carrots

50g (1³/₄oz) each, diced celery and spring onion

20g (³/₄oz) diced parsley root

20g (³/₄oz) plain flour

sea salt and freshly ground black pepper

1 litre (1³/₄ pints) chicken stock

2 garlic cloves, finely chopped

1 bay leaf

5 black peppercorns

120ml (4fl oz) single cream

6 tbsp chopped mixed herbs, such as dill, sage, basil, parsley, chervil, sorrel, lovage, oregano, thyme, or chives, in any combination

METHOD

1 Place a medium pan over low heat and add 1 tbsp butter. Add the onion, cover, and leave to sweat for about 5–10 minutes. Add the vegetables and stir to coat in butter. Cover and sweat until softened, for about 5–10 minutes.

2 Sprinkle the flour over the vegetables and give them a stir. Season lightly, then pour in the stock stirring. Raise the heat to high and bring the soup to a boil.

3 When it is boiling, turn down the heat and add the garlic, bay leaf, and peppercorns. Simmer uncovered for about 30 minutes. Skim off any froth.

4 Stir in the cream. Turn up the heat but do not boil. After 5 minutes, remove from the heat and strain the soup into a large bowl. Discard the vegetables and spices. Pour the soup back into the pan. Whisk in the remaining butter and add the herbs, keeping some back to finish. Simmer for 5 minutes, stirring occasionally. Season to taste, spoon into bowls, garnish with herbs and serve.

Freeze herbs

Freezing fresh herbs is a useful way to preserve them, and they retain a flavour for cooking that is almost as good as fresh. There are several easy ways of doing this. Make a mix of herbs and oil and spoon into freezer bags, or freeze with a little water in ice cube trays for use in pestos, sauces, and soups. Herb butters can add a fresh, aromatic touch to grilled or fried meats. Simply slice into rounds as needed straight from the fridge or freezer.

Herb oil mixes

1 **Chop the herbs and add oil** Coarsely chop the herbs in a food processor. Whizz briefly with the motor running and add enough olive oil to lightly coat the herbs.

2 **Store in freezer** Spoon the mixture into small freezer bags, seal them securely, label, and place in the freezer. Herbs in oil can be frozen for up to 4 months.

Quick herb butters

Many different herbs and combinations of herbs work as butters. Here are a few suggestions:

Watercress butter Combine watercress leaves with butter, seasoning, and lemon juice for a peppery butter to go with grilled meats and fish.

Parsley butter Combine butter with parsley, lemon juice, garlic, and seasoning for a butter that goes wonderfully well with chicken, fish, and snails.

Spinach and shallot butter Make a simple butter with chopped spinach leaves, shallots, some parsley,

chervil, and tarragon. This is an ideal accompaniment to soups and bisques.

Oregano butter Add oregano, olive oil, and garlic to butter for a Mediterranean flavour.

Tarragon butter Mix tarragon, lemon juice, seasoning, and butter to enjoy with white fish.

Herb ice cubes

Freeze the cubes Fill an ice cube tray with herbs and pour water over to cover. Freeze until solid, for about 2 hours. Store in labelled freezer bags until needed. Use within 6 months.

Herb butters

Store the butter Combine chopped herbs and soft butter, shape into a sausage, wrap in cling film, and twist the ends to seal. Keep in the fridge for 1 week or in the freezer for 3 months.

PARSLEY

When to pick
Pick both flat-leaf and curly parsley when the leaves are dark green and glossy, and before they become too large. Pick frequently to encourage regrowth.

Eat and store fresh
Keep parsley in a glass of water, in or out of the fridge, or wrapped in damp kitchen paper in the fridge for 3–4 days. Use fresh whenever possible. Often used in soups and stews.

How to preserve
Use parsley in a pesto and store in the fridge for up to 2 weeks. Alternatively, dry the leaves flat or hang them to dry for 2 weeks, then store in sealed glass jars for up to 6 months (see pages 160–1).

Freezing options
Freeze in a herb butter or by adding oil and putting into freezer bags, or by freezing in ice cubes (see pages 148–9).

This Mediterranean favourite is particularly good served with poached chicken or salmon, or grilled tuna. Change the amount and type of herbs you use, depending on what is available.

Sauce verte

Makes 240ml (8fl oz) • **Prep** 20 mins

INGREDIENTS

1 tbsp fresh breadcrumbs, made from day-old bread

1 tbsp white wine vinegar

1 tsp Dijon mustard

175ml (6fl oz) extra virgin olive oil

5 tbsp finely chopped flat-leaf or curly parsley, plus stalks (optional)

3 tbsp finely chopped basil

1 tbsp finely chopped mint

2 garlic cloves, crushed

2 anchovy fillets, chopped

2 tbsp capers, drained, and finely chopped

2–3 tbsp lemon juice, and 2 tsp finely grated unwaxed lemon zest

sea salt and freshly ground black pepper

METHOD

1 In a bowl, mix the breadcrumbs and vinegar together with the mustard and 3 tbsp of the olive oil.

2 Add the herbs, reserving 1 heaped tbsp of the mixed herbs to finish, and beat well. If you like, chop a few parsley stalks very finely and stir them in for extra flavour.

3 Add the garlic, anchovies, and half the capers, and beat again. The mixture will become a very thick green paste.

4 Gradually beat in the rest of the olive oil a little at a time, and then season to taste with salt and pepper. Shortly before serving, stir in the lemon juice and zest, and add the reserved herbs and capers. Use soon or cover, chill, and use within 24 hours.

Tabbouleh, a herby Middle Eastern salad, is always more about the herbs than it is about the bulghur wheat. In this recipe the handfuls of fresh herbs used produce a truly flavourful result.

Herbed tabbouleh

Serves 4 • **Prep** 25 mins

INGREDIENTS

For the dressing

1 garlic clove, crushed

sea salt

$^1/_2$ tsp five-spice powder

1 tbsp lemon juice and
    1 tsp finely grated
    lemon zest

1 tbsp pomegranate molasses
    or balsamic vinegar

4 tbsp extra virgin olive oil

freshly ground black pepper

For the salad

75g (2$^1/_2$oz) fine bulghur wheat

6 tbsp chopped
    flat-leaf parsley

1 tbsp finely chopped mint

1 tbsp chopped coriander

4 spring onions, finely chopped

4 baby cherry
    tomatoes, chopped

METHOD

1 In a bowl, mix the garlic with a little salt, the five-spice powder, lemon juice and zest, and the pomegranate molasses or balsamic vinegar. Whisk in the olive oil and season with salt and pepper to taste. Leave it to stand while you prepare the ingredients for the salad.

2 Put the bulghur in a shallow bowl, cover with boiling water, and leave to swell for 2 minutes. Tip into a sieve, drain, and refresh with plenty of cold water, rubbing the bulghur grains between your fingers. Shake the bulghur and then drain it well.

3 Tip the bulghur into the bowl with the dressing mixture. Add the parsley, mint, coriander, spring onions, and tomatoes. Toss just before serving and season with salt and pepper.

Variation You can add 2 or 3 tbsp pomegranate seeds for a crunchy, jewel-like finish.

Also called Arabic salad, this dish is popular in Turkey and the Middle East. Laden with fresh herbs and spices, it's a perfect foil for some grilled or barbecued lamb, or lemony chicken.

Shepherd's salad

Serves 4 • **Prep** 20 mins

INGREDIENTS

For the dressing

1/2 garlic clove, crushed

1/2 tsp sweet paprika

1/2 tsp ground sumac

1/2 tsp caster sugar

1/2 tsp ground cumin

2 tbsp lemon juice and
    1 tsp grated lemon zest

7 tbsp extra virgin olive oil

sea salt and freshly ground
    black pepper

For the salad

1 large cucumber, peeled

15 baby cherry tomatoes

1 head sweet romaine lettuce

12 black olives, pitted
    and chopped

3 spring onions, chopped

2 tbsp each chopped flat-leaf
    parsley, coriander, and mint

2 tbsp chopped purslane
    or rocket

METHOD

1 In a bowl, mix all the ingredients for the dressing, and season with salt and pepper to taste. Leave the mixture to rest while you prepare the salad ingredients.

2 Cut the cucumber into 4 segments lengthways, scoop out the seeds, and discard them. Cut the flesh into small, neat chunks. Reserve on a plate. Halve the tomatoes, scoop out and discard some of the seeds, and add to the cucumber. Tear or chop the lettuce into bite-sized pieces.

3 Stir the dressing. Put a layer of lettuce in the bowl (do not toss), scatter in some olives and spring onion, and sprinkle in some parsley, purslane or wild rocket, coriander, and mint. Add half the cucumber and tomatoes. Continue adding the ingredients until everything is in the bowl.

4 Toss the salad just before serving.

153

Dry herbs

The flavour of herbs with woody stalks and tougher leaves, such as bay, thyme, and rosemary is well preserved by drying. Place individual leaves, fronds, and small sprigs on a piece of muslin stretched over a frame out of direct sunlight in a dry, airy room for at least 2 weeks until their colour fades a little and the herbs turn slightly brittle. Alternatively, hang in bundles to dry. Most home-dried herbs lose their flavour after 6 months as their essential oils evaporate.

Drying flat

1 **Lay herbs flat** Place leaves of herbs such as thyme, rosemary, marjoram, oregano, fennel, dill, bay, or sage, flat on a muslin cloth so they do not touch one another.

2 **Store in jars** Once dry (leave for at least 2 weeks) pack the herbs loosely in clean glass jars with tightly fitting lids. Seal the jars and store away from direct light.

Drying seeds and flowers

Fennel, dill, and coriander seeds, among others, can be home-dried for use in cooking. Both dried seeds and flowers should be used within 6 months.

Seeds Hang up bunches of stems, covering the seed heads with muslin and tying securely in place. After a week or so collect the seeds and store in a paper bag.

Flowers Lavender, fennel, and chamomile flowers are easy to dry. Remove the stems, cut off the flowers, and dry on a muslin stretched over a frame for 3 weeks.

Hanging herbs

1 Make herb posies Tie together 3–4 stems of single herbs, such as bay, fennel fronds, rosemary, or thyme. Hang in an airy, dry room out of direct sunlight.

2 Leave to dry Hang strips of lemon peel alongside the herbs, if you like, and leave for 2 weeks until the colour fades and the herbs are brittle. Untie and store in sealed jars.

161

MINT

When to pick
Pick the bigger leaves, to allow the smaller ones to develop. Pinch off sprigs just above a set of leaves, to encourage regrowth. Whole stems can also be picked.

Eat and store fresh
Keep mint in a glass of water or damp kitchen paper in the fridge for 2–3 days. Use with new potatoes, courgettes, and peas, and to make mint tea.

How to preserve
Combine with vinegar and sugar for mint sauce. Dry leaves flat on muslin for 2 weeks then store in sealed glass jars for up to 6 months (see pages 160–1).

Freezing options
Freeze in a herb butter, or coarsely chop in oil and spoon into individual freezer bags, or freeze in ice cubes before transferring to bags (see pages 148–9).

This cordial has a delicate menthol flavour. For a stronger taste, try doubling the quantity of mint leaves used. To serve, dilute with still or sparkling mineral water, or use as a base for cocktails.

Fresh mint cordial

Makes approx. 400ml (14fl oz) • **Prep** 20 mins, plus infusing • **Cooking** 5 mins

INGREDIENTS

50g (1³/₄oz) peppermint,
    Moroccan mint,
    or spearmint
    (garden mint) leaves
300g (10¹/₂oz) caster sugar
a few drops of natural green
    food colouring
a few drops of natural
    peppermint extract
    (only if using spearmint)

METHOD

1 Put the mint leaves in a large bowl, add the sugar, and pound with the end of a rolling pin or a pestle to bruise and crush them to a paste.

2 Pour over 300ml (10fl oz) of boiling water, stir, cover, and leave to infuse for at least 2 hours or until the mixture is completely cold.

3 Strain through a sieve into a saucepan, pressing and squeezing the mint to extract the maximum flavour. Heat the pan over moderate heat, stirring until the sugar has dissolved. Then boil for 2 minutes. Stir in a few drops of natural green food colouring and peppermint extract (if using).

4 Pour immediately into a warm sterilized bottle using a sterilized funnel. Seal, label, and leave to cool, then store in the fridge. Shake before use.

A lovely addition to fruity summer drinks and cocktails. Try diluting this delicate syrup with mineral water or pouring it over vanilla ice cream for an instant dessert.

Mint and orange syrup

Makes approx. 250ml (8fl oz) or 1 small bottle • **Prep** 15 mins • **Cooking** 20 mins

INGREDIENTS

5 tbsp chopped mint,
    preferably Moroccan mint
grated zest of 1–2 large
    unwaxed oranges
300g (10$\frac{1}{2}$oz) caster sugar
100ml (3$\frac{1}{2}$fl oz) orange juice,
    freshly squeezed
2 tbsp Cointreau or any
    other orange liqueur

METHOD

1 Put the mint and grated orange zest in a double layer of muslin, bring up the edges, and tie with string. Put the sugar, orange juice, orange liqueur, and 200ml (7fl oz) water into a pan, and add the muslin bag.

2 Bring to a boil over moderate heat, stirring occasionally until the sugar has dissolved. Leave to simmer for 5–7 minutes, stirring from time to time until the syrup has thickened just a little.

3 Remove from the heat, cover, and leave to cool. Lift out the muslin bag and squeeze it over the pan to extract as much flavour as possible, then discard it. Strain the syrup through a fine sieve, lined with dampened muslin, into a warm sterilized bottle and seal.

Note Store in a cool place and use within 4–6 weeks.

This pretty, aromatic syrup is delicious poured over roasted peaches and served with Greek-style yogurt or crème fraîche. It works equally well when flavouring meringues, cakes, and biscuits.

Lavender syrup

Makes 200–250ml (7–8fl oz) • **Prep** 15 mins • **Cooking** 15 mins, plus infusing

INGREDIENTS

2 tsp dried lavender flowers
300g (10$\frac{1}{2}$oz) caster sugar
pared zest of 1 small unwaxed
    lemon, cut into small strips

METHOD

1 Put the dried lavender flowers, sugar, and lemon zest strips into a saucepan with 300ml (10fl oz) water. Place over medium heat and stir.

2 Once the sugar has dissolved after 3–4 minutes, stop stirring and remove from the heat. Leave to infuse for at least 30 minutes, stirring occasionally.

3 Return the pan to medium heat and bring to a boil without stirring. Turn the heat to high and let the syrup bubble for 5–7 minutes until thickened.

4 Remove from the heat. When the syrup is cool enough to handle, strain slowly and carefully into a warm sterilized bottle through a fine sieve, lined with dampened muslin. Leave until completely cold before sealing.

Note Store in a cool place and use within 4–6 weeks.

LAVENDER

When to pick
Pick the flower heads or stems of lavender (if drying) when they first open. The leaves can be picked at any time and used sparingly for cooking.

Eat and store fresh
Lavender can be stored in a glass of water, in or out of the fridge, for up to 5 days. Use the leaves like rosemary to accompany roast lamb, and the flowers add a wonderful aroma to baked goods.

How to preserve
Dry the picked flower heads on muslin for 3 weeks and store in sealed glass jars for up to 6 months (see pages 160–1), or tie whole bunches with string and hang up to dry.

Freezing options
Freeze chopped flowers with water in ice cube trays, and use in drinks and to flavour syrups, custards, jellies, and baked goods.

GOOSEBERRIES

When to pick

Pick gooseberries when young and tart for cooking. Leave dessert varieties to grow plump for eating raw. Always net gooseberries to stop birds feasting on them.

Eat and store fresh

Cook young gooseberries over gentle heat with a little sugar. Dessert gooseberries taste delicious in a fruit salad. Store in the fridge for up to 3 days.

How to preserve

Preserve gooseberries in jams, jellies, and chutneys. They can also be bottled or used in cordials or for home brewing.

Freezing options

Open freeze whole on trays, as a cooked or uncooked purée, as a freezer jam (see pages 176–7), or blanched or poached in sugar syrup (see pages 194–5).

Like a dessert from the 1950s, this gooseberry tart has all the delicacy and demure simplicity of a bygone age. The gooseberries quiver in the just-set custard, all held together in a light pastry.

Gooseberry tart

Serves 6–8 • **Prep** 30 mins, plus chilling • **Cooking** 1 hour 10 mins

INGREDIENTS

400g (14oz) gooseberries
250ml (8fl oz) double cream
2 eggs
50g (1³/₄oz) caster sugar

For the pastry

150g (5¹/₂oz) plain flour
25g (scant 1 oz) caster sugar
75g (2¹/₂oz) butter
1 egg yolk

or 250g (9 oz) ready-made shortcrust pastry

METHOD

1 For the pastry, combine the flour, sugar, and butter, and mix in a food processor to form fine breadcrumbs. Add the egg yolk and process until the mixture forms a ball, adding a little cold water, a tablespoon at a time, if necessary. Wrap the pastry in cling film and leave it in the fridge to chill for 30 minutes.

2 Preheat the oven to 180°C (350°F/Gas 4). Meanwhile, top and tail the gooseberries and set aside. To make the custard, whisk together the cream, eggs, and sugar in a bowl. Put the custard in the fridge.

3 Roll out the pastry into a circle a little larger than a 24cm (10in) loose-bottomed tart tin. Line the tart tin with the pastry. Line the pastry case with greaseproof paper and baking beans, and bake blind for 15 minutes. Remove the beans and paper, and bake for another 10 minutes until cooked through but still pale.

4 Remove the tin from the oven and put a single layer of gooseberries in the pastry case. Pour the custard over and return it to the oven for a further 35 minutes until the custard is set and golden at the edges. Leave to cool slightly before serving with some thick cream or custard.

An all-time favourite treatment for gooseberries, this chilled dessert is the epitome of summer eating. Try freezing the chilled purée so you can make this delicious fool whenever you like.

Gooseberry fool
with elderflower

Serves 4–6 • **Prep** 20 mins, plus chilling • **Cooking** 10 mins

INGREDIENTS

350g (12oz) gooseberries,
   topped and tailed
100g (3½oz) caster sugar
1 tbsp elderflower cordial
240g (8½oz) good quality
   ready-made custard
200ml (7fl oz) double cream

METHOD

1 Put the gooseberries, sugar, and elderflower cordial into a pan and stir to dissolve the sugar. Cover and cook over low heat for 5 minutes until the gooseberries have given out some water and started to swell. Remove the lid and cook for another 5 minutes.

2 Mash the gooseberries lightly with a potato masher to break up a few of the bigger ones. Alternatively, if you prefer a smoother fool, purée the fruit in a blender or food processor. Leave the mixture to cool completely, and then chill in the fridge.

3 In a large bowl, whip the double cream until it forms fairly stiff peaks.

4 Once the purée is completely cold, remove it from the fridge, fold it into the cream, and then fold in the cold custard to make a light, fluffy fool. Spoon into a serving dish or individual glasses and chill in the fridge for a few hours, or overnight, before serving.

Granitas are much simpler to make than ice cream and far more virtuous in the calorie count. Try this classic pairing of red summer berries for a refreshing iced dessert.

Red berry granita

Serves 6 • **Prep** 10 mins, plus freezing

INGREDIENTS

125g (4^1/$_2$oz) icing sugar
1 tbsp lemon juice
250g (9oz) strawberries, hulled
250g (9oz) raspberries
single cream, to serve (optional)

METHOD

1 Put the sugar and lemon juice in a blender or food processor with 150ml (5fl oz) boiling water and whizz until the sugar has all dissolved. Add the strawberries and raspberries, and process to a purée.

2 Transfer the mixture to a shallow freezer-proof plastic container, cover, and place in the freezer for 4 hours. Remove from the freezer every hour and stir with a fork, breaking the mixture up into small pieces. When the mixture has completely broken up into frozen, gravelly pieces, serve straight from the freezer on its own, or with a drizzle of single cream.

Note The granita can be kept in the freezer for up to 1 month.

STRAWBERRIES

When to pick
Pick strawberries when dark red, firm, and glossy. Pick them with the hull and a little stalk intact as they will store longer. Harvest small fruits for jam or ice cream.

Eat and store fresh
Eat strawberries as soon as possible after picking. Keep them for up to 2 days in the fridge, and bring back to room temperature before eating.

How to preserve
A classic fruit for jam, strawberries can also be used to make cordials and syrups, and can be bottled.

Freezing options
Open freeze whole on trays, as a cooked or uncooked purée, as a freezer jam (see pages 176–7), or blanched or poached in sugar syrup (see pages 194–5).

If you're looking for new and interesting ways of using your crop of home-grown strawberries, this frozen dessert is a delicious alternative to eating them simply with cream and sugar.

Strawberry semifreddo

Serves 6–8 • **Prep** 20 mins, plus freezing

INGREDIENTS

225g (8oz) strawberries, hulled, plus extra whole strawberries and redcurrants to decorate
250ml (8fl oz) double cream
50g (1³⁄₄oz) icing sugar
115g (4oz) ready-made meringues, coarsely crushed
3 tbsp raspberry-flavoured liqueur

For the coulis

225g (8oz) strawberries, hulled
30–50g (1–1³⁄₄oz) icing sugar
1–2 tsp lemon juice, brandy, grappa, or balsamic vinegar

METHOD

1 Lightly brush a 20cm (8in) loose-bottomed, springform tin with vegetable oil, then line the base with greaseproof paper and set aside.

2 Purée the strawberries in a blender or food processor. Whip the cream with the icing sugar until it just holds its shape. Fold the strawberry purée and cream together, then fold in the crushed meringues and liqueur. Turn the mixture into the tin, smooth the surface, cover with cling film, and freeze for at least 6 hours, or overnight.

3 Meanwhile, make the strawberry coulis. Purée the strawberries in a blender or food processor, then press them through a fine sieve to remove the seeds. Stir 25g (scant 1oz) icing sugar into the purée and taste for sweetness, adding more sugar if necessary. Flavour the coulis with the lemon juice.

4 Just before serving, remove the semifreddo from the tin, peel away the lining paper, and using a warmed knife, cut into slices. Arrange the slices on individual plates, spoon the coulis around the base, and decorate with whole strawberries and redcurrants.

Note Store in the freezer for up to 3 months.

This delicate cake is a delicious twist on a baking classic. Adding fresh strawberries to the traditional filling gives it a summery elegance.

Victoria sandwich
with strawberries and cream

Serves 8 • **Prep** 20 mins • **Cooking** 25 mins

INGREDIENTS

225g (8oz) butter, at
    room temperature
225g (8oz) caster sugar
4 large eggs, lightly beaten
225g (8oz) self-raising flour

For the filling
100ml (3$^{1}/_{2}$oz) double cream
175g (6oz) strawberries,
    hulled and sliced
icing sugar, to dust

METHOD

1 Preheat the oven to 180°C (350°F/Gas 4). Line the base of two 20cm (8in) sandwich tins with baking parchment. In a bowl, mix the butter and sugar with an electric hand whisk until light and creamy.

2 Whisk in the eggs a little at a time, adding in a little of the flour if the mixture looks as if it is going to curdle.

3 Sift in the remaining flour and fold in gently with a large metal spoon. Divide the mixture between the tins and bake for 25 minutes, or until risen and firm to the touch. Leave to cool in the tins for 5 minutes, then transfer to a wire rack to cool completely.

4 To make the filling, place the cream in a bowl and whisk with an electric hand whisk until soft peaks form. Spread over one of the cakes, then top with strawberries. Place the other cake on top, then dust thickly with icing sugar.

These delightful little cakes are perfect served with afternoon tea. For a party canapé, cut smaller versions, sandwich with a single slice of strawberry, and serve to your guests.

Chocolate strawberry
shortcakes

Serves 6 • **Prep** 15 mins • **Cooking** 10 mins

INGREDIENTS

200g (7oz) plain flour

30g (1oz) cocoa powder

2 tsp baking powder

60g (2oz) butter, at room
    temperature

60g (2oz) caster sugar, plus
    extra for sweetening

1 large egg

1 tsp natural vanilla extract

6 tbsp milk

225g (8oz) strawberries

150ml (5fl oz) double
    cream, whipped

METHOD

1 Preheat the oven to 230°C (450°F/Gas 8). Sift the flour, cocoa, and baking powder into a bowl. Add the butter and rub in with fingertips. Stir in the sugar. Beat the egg with the vanilla and stir in. Add enough milk to form a soft, but not sticky, dough. Knead gently until smooth.

2 Pat out the dough to about 1cm (¹/₂in) thick. Cut into 6 rounds using a 7.5cm (3in) cutter. Place on a lightly greased baking sheet. Bake in the oven for about 10 minutes until risen and the bases sound hollow when tapped. Transfer to a wire rack to cool for 5–10 minutes.

3 Halve 3 strawberries for decoration, leaving the calyces intact, and reserve. Hull and slice the remaining strawberries in half, and sweeten with a little caster sugar, if necessary.

4 Split the shortcakes, sandwich with the sliced strawberries and some of the cream. Top with the remaining cream and decorate with the reserved, halved strawberries.

This classic soft-set conserve is for those times when you have so many strawberries that you just can't eat them all. Steeping the fruit in sugar stops them breaking up too much while cooking.

Strawberry conserve

Makes 3 medium jars • **Prep** 20 mins, plus standing • **Cooking** 25 mins

INGREDIENTS

900g (2lb) juicy
    strawberries, hulled
900g (2lb) granulated sugar
juice of 1 lemon
juice of 1 lime

METHOD

1 Layer the strawberries and sugar in a large bowl, cover, and leave for several hours or overnight.

2 Tip the fruit and sugar into a preserving pan or a large heavy saucepan. Cook over low heat, stirring continuously, until the sugar has all dissolved. Then boil gently for about 5 minutes, just enough for the fruit to soften but not to break up too much. Remove the pan from the heat, cover it loosely with some muslin, and leave the cooked fruit overnight.

3 Remove the muslin, put the pan back on the heat, stir in the lemon and lime juice and bring to a boil. Boil gently for 5–10 minutes or until thickened and the setting point is reached, skimming off any scum from the surface, as needed. Remove the pan from the heat while you test for a set (see pages 186–7).

4 Ladle into warm sterilized jars, cover with discs of waxed paper, seal, and label.

Note Keeps for 6 months. Store in a cool, dark place, and refrigerate after opening.

Make freezer jam

Uncooked freezer jams are a great solution
for anyone who wants fresh-tasting, low-sugar
spreads. Very ripe, juicy fruits, especially those
low in pectin and acid, are difficult to set properly
as traditional jam (see pages 186–7), but are ideal
as thickened purées. This method uses agar, a healthy,
tasteless, Japanese gelling agent which gives these quick
jams a jelly-like set. They can be used thawed on toast, desserts, or yogurt.
Once thawed and opened, freezer jams should be used within 2 weeks.

1 **Crush berries** Wash the strawberries
briefly, put them into a large bowl with
the lemon juice, and crush with the back
of a fork to a rough purée.

2 **Add the agar and simmer** Put 250ml
(8fl oz) cold water in a pan. Add the agar.
Leave for 3 minutes, bring to a boil, and
simmer for 5. Add the sugar and stir to dissolve.

Recipe Strawberry freezer jam

Makes approx. 600g (1lb 5oz) • **Prep** 15 mins, plus standing • **Keeps** 6 months

INGREDIENTS

500g (1lb 2oz) ripe
   strawberries at
   room temperature
1 tbsp lemon juice

1 tbsp agar flakes
   or 1 tsp agar powder
60–115g (2–4oz)
   caster sugar

Other fruits for freezer jams

Using the basic recipe shown here, make freezer jams using any of the fruits below.

Blackberries Add a little mixed spice for a delicious autumn jam.
Blueberries Use on their own or with other fruits such as raspberries (see page 183).
Cherries Halve and stone the fruit first.

Also suitable for freezer jams:
Figs, nectarines, melons, peaches, pears, raspberries, and tayberries.

3 **Add to the fruit** Pour the hot agar syrup onto the fruit, stirring constantly until it is well mixed (use a rubber spatula to scrape all the syrup out of the pan).

4 **Pot and store** Pour the jam into clean freezer pots, leaving room for expansion. Leave to cool, then seal, leave in the fridge overnight to thicken fully, and freeze.

177

RASPBERRIES

When to pick
Pick all varieties of raspberries when a deep colour, but before they go too soft. They should be sweet to taste and should come away from the plant easily.

Eat and store fresh
Eat as soon as possible after picking. They will keep for 2 days in the fridge, but need to be brought back to room temperature before eating. If cooking, raspberries can be kept in the fridge for up to 3 days.

How to preserve
Delicious in jams and cordials, raspberries can also be bottled or made into fruit curds and cheese.

Freezing options
Open freeze whole on trays, as a cooked or uncooked purée, as a freezer jam (see pages 176–7), or blanched or poached in sugar syrup (see pages 194–5).

A delicate and impressive looking take on the traditional brûlée. Raspberries can lose some of their freshness when cooked, but the ground hazelnuts in this dessert act to enhance their flavour.

Raspberry and hazelnut
crème brûlée

Serves 4 • **Prep** 10 mins, plus chilling • **Cooking** 30 mins

INGREDIENTS

115g (4oz) raspberries
140g (5oz) caster sugar
1 tsp finely grated lemon zest
400ml (14fl oz) double cream
2 eggs
60g (2oz) ground hazelnuts
$\frac{1}{2}$ tsp natural vanilla extract

METHOD

1 Divide the raspberries between 4 ramekins. Sprinkle with 1 tbsp of the sugar and the lemon zest.

2 Whisk the cream with the eggs, hazelnuts, vanilla extract, and 1 tbsp of the sugar. Pour over the raspberries. Stand the dishes in a large frying pan with enough boiling water to come halfway up the sides of the dishes. Cover the pan with a lid or foil and cook very gently for about 30 minutes or until set. Don't let the water boil or the custard will curdle. Leave to cool, then chill in the fridge.

3 Remove from the fridge, sprinkle liberally with the remaining sugar and grill under high heat for 3–4 minutes until caramelized. Alternatively, move a cook's blow torch over the surface to caramelize the sugar. Leave to stand for 5 minutes, then serve.

This fragrant dessert is a perfect finale to a summer meal. Fresh raspberries are so delicious that I mostly eat them straight from the garden, yet an elegant recipe like this shows them at their best.

Cold raspberry soufflé

Serves 4 • **Prep** 30 mins

INGREDIENTS

1 tbsp sunflower oil
4 tbsp rosewater
1 tbsp powdered gelatine
350g (12oz) raspberries
1 tbsp lemon juice
85g (3oz) icing sugar, sieved
450ml (15fl oz) double cream
4 egg whites
mint leaves, to garnish

METHOD

1 Wrap double-layered bands of greaseproof paper around the outsides of 4 ramekins so they sit 5cm (2in) above the rim. Secure with adhesive tape. Brush the inside rim of the paper lightly with oil.

2 Place the rosewater in a small bowl, sprinkle with the gelatine, and leave to soak for 2 minutes, or until it becomes spongy. Set the bowl in a larger bowl, half filled with boiling water, and stir to dissolve the gelatine. Remove from the heat and allow to cool slightly.

3 Place all but 8 of the raspberries in a food processor and blend to a purée. Sieve, discarding any pips. Stir in the lemon juice and sugar, then stir in the gelatine. Leave in a cool place until just beginning to set.

4 Whip the cream to soft peaks and fold into the raspberry mixture. In a separate bowl, whisk the egg whites until stiff and fold into the raspberry mixture. Pour into the ramekins and chill in the fridge until set.

5 Remove from the fridge, peel off the greaseproof paper from each ramekin and decorate with the reserved whole raspberries and mint leaves.

Soft fruit such as berries do not keep for long after picking. One way to preserve their juicy freshness is by turning them into these tempting ice lollies to bring out later in the year.

Fruit lollies

Makes 4–6 small lollies • **Prep** 20 mins, plus freezing • **Cooking** 5 mins

INGREDIENTS

115g (4oz) caster sugar
500g (1lb 2oz) ripe berries
such as raspberries,
strawberries, or
blackberries, washed
juice of 1 lemon

METHOD

1 First make a sugar syrup by placing the sugar and 120ml (4fl oz) of water in a heavy saucepan. Place the pan over low heat and stir the mixture with a wooden spoon until the sugar has dissolved.

2 Cook the syrup on medium to high heat to achieve a steady boil for 1–2 minutes. Then turn off the heat and allow the syrup to cool.

3 Purée the berries by passing them through a sieve, discarding any seeds. If the fruit is too hard to go through the sieve easily, blitz it with a hand blender or in a food processor to make a purée first, then sieve.

4 Add the lemon juice and sugar syrup to the bowl and mix them into the berry purée.

5 Pour the mixture into ice lolly moulds, slot an ice lolly stick into each mould (if needed), and freeze.

Note These will keep in the freezer for up to 6 months.

A lovely, light cake that is equally good eaten warm or cold. Although it suits tea in the garden on a summer's day, it would also work as a dessert, served warm with cream.

Raspberry bake
with lemon and almonds

Serves 8 • **Prep** 20 mins • **Cooking** 40 mins

INGREDIENTS

125g (4$\frac{1}{2}$oz) plain flour

1 tsp baking powder

75g (2$\frac{1}{2}$oz) ground almonds

150g (5$\frac{1}{2}$oz) butter, cubed

200g (7oz) caster sugar

juice of 1 lemon

1 tsp natural vanilla extract

2 large eggs

200g (7oz) fresh raspberries

icing sugar, to dust

METHOD

1 Preheat the oven to 180°C (350°F/Gas 4). Line the base and sides of a 20cm (8in) loose-bottomed cake tin with greaseproof paper.

2 Sift the flour into a bowl, add the baking powder and ground almonds, and mix well. In a pan, melt the butter, sugar, and lemon juice together, stirring until well combined.

3 Stir this syrupy mixture into the dry ingredients, then whisk in the vanilla extract and the eggs, one at a time, until the mixture is smooth and well combined. Pour into the tin, then scatter the raspberries over the top. Bake for 35–40 minutes, or until golden and a skewer inserted into the cake comes out clean.

4 Cool in the tin for 10 minutes, then turn out and cool completely on a wire rack. Dust with icing sugar and cut into rectangles to serve.

This easy-to-make jam is wonderful served with thick, tangy yogurt as a low-fat dessert or at breakfast. To use, thaw overnight in the fridge, then keep refrigerated and use within two weeks.

Raspberry and blueberry
quick freezer jam

Makes approx. 500g (1lb 2oz) • **Prep** 10 mins • **Cooking** 12 mins

INGREDIENTS

225g (8oz) raspberries and
    225g (8oz) blueberries,
    at room temperature
2 tsp lemon juice
1 tbsp agar flakes or
    1 tsp agar powder
115g (4oz) caster sugar

METHOD

1 Put the fruit in a bowl with the lemon juice and roughly crush with a potato masher or fork; leave some texture, rather than reducing the berries to a smooth pulp.

2 Put 200ml (7fl oz) of water in a small saucepan, sprinkle the agar flakes or powder over it, and leave to soften for 2–3 minutes. Give the pan a gentle swirl, then bring the water slowly to a boil over low heat, without stirring it. Simmer gently for 3–5 minutes, stirring occasionally to make sure all the agar has dissolved.

3 Add the sugar and stir for 2–3 minutes over low heat until dissolved. Remove from the heat.

4 Pour the hot agar syrup over the fruit in the bowl, stirring the fruit gently and constantly until the ingredients are well mixed. Pour into clean freezer pots, leaving 1cm ($\frac{1}{2}$in) space at the top. Leave to cool, then seal and label. Leave overnight in the fridge to thicken fully, then freeze.

Note Keeps for 6 months in the freezer.

Sometimes called jumbleberry jam, this can be made with any juicy summer fruits, though raspberries are essential. Try blackberries, blackcurrants, redcurrants, or cherries in the mix.

Mixed berry jam

Makes approx. 350g (12oz) or 1 medium jar • **Prep** 10 mins • **Cooking** 15 mins

INGREDIENTS

450g (1lb) mix of raspberries, strawberries, and blueberries, hulled if needed
450g (1lb) caster or granulated sugar
juice of 2 lemons

METHOD

1 Put the fruit in a preserving pan or a large heavy saucepan and lightly crush it with the back of a wooden spoon.

2 Add the sugar and heat gently, stirring until all the sugar has dissolved. Turn up the heat and bring to a boil. When the jam reaches a rolling boil, cook for 5–10 minutes or until it reaches the setting point. Remove the pan from the heat while you test for a set (see pages 186–7).

3 Use a skimmer to skim off any surface scum. Leave the jam to cool slightly so that a thin skin forms and the berries are evenly distributed throughout the jam. Ladle into a warm sterilized jar, cover with a waxed paper disc, seal, and label.

Note Keeps for 6–9 months. Store in a cool, dark place, and refrigerate after opening.

Make fruit jam

Jams are the simplest of preserves where fruit is cooked with sugar over high heat until set. This method, suitable for all soft-skinned berries, produces a soft-set jam. Once opened, refrigerate and use within 3 to 4 weeks. It is important to get the correct balance of sugar, acid, and naturally-occurring pectin as this helps the jam set. Some fruits, such as plums, have high pectin content. Others, including cherries and pears, that have low levels need extra pectin added. Raspberries are a medium-pectin fruit and the lemon juice helps to achieve a set.

1 **Simmer fruit** Wash the fruit and put in a preserving pan or large heavy saucepan. Add the lemon juice and water. Simmer gently for 3–5 minutes, add the sugar, and stir.

2 **Bring to a boil** Turn up the heat and bring the jam to a rolling boil for 5–10 minutes or until a setting point is reached. Take the pan off the heat to test for a set.

Recipe Raspberry jam

Makes approx. 450g (1lb) or 2 small jars
Prep 15 mins • **Keeps** 6 months

INGREDIENTS

650g (1½lb) raspberries

juice of ½ lemon

150ml (5fl oz) water

500g (1lb 2oz) caster or
    granulated sugar

Tips on making fruit jams

When you think your jam has reached its
setting point, you must test for a set.

Testing for a set Usually jams and conserves
take 5–20 minutes, jellies 5–15 minutes, and
marmalades 10–30 minutes to set. Remove the
pan from the heat and follow step 3 below.

Sterilize bottles and jars To ensure successful
preservation sterilize all jars, bottles, and lids
just before you need them. Wash in hot water,
drain upside down, and put in a cool oven
(140°C/275°F/Gas 1) for 15 minutes.

3 **Testing for a set** Put 1 tsp of jam on
a chilled saucer, allow to cool, then push
across it with your finger. If your finger
leaves a trail and the jam wrinkles, it is set.

4 **Put in jars and store** Ladle the jam
into warm sterilized jars using a sterilized
jam funnel. Cover with waxed paper,
seal, label, and store in a cool, dark place.

When to pick

Pick blackberries when the fruits are dark purple, glossy, and sweet to taste. Slightly under-ripe berries are better for making jam.

Eat and store fresh

If eating raw, use blackberries within 2 days of picking and eat at room temperature. If cooking, they will keep for up to 3 days in the fridge before using.

How to preserve

Preserve blackberries in jams or jellies. Wild blackberries are often woody, and are better made into jelly. They can also be used in chutneys and fruit cheeses.

Freezing options

Open freeze whole on trays, as a cooked or uncooked purée, as a freezer jam (see pages 176–7), or blanched or poached in sugar syrup (see pages 194–5).

This is the ultimate in fast desserts, yet it looks impressive and is incredibly tasty. It is pleasing to think that an afternoon's blackberry picking can give such rewarding results.

Blackberry brioche
with mascarpone

Serves 4 • **Prep** 5 mins • **Cooking** 10 mins

INGREDIENTS

50g (1³/₄oz) butter

50g (1³/₄oz) caster sugar

400g (14oz) blackberries

4–8 slices of brioche

200g (7oz) mascarpone cheese

METHOD

1 Melt the butter in a frying pan. Add the sugar and allow it to melt and start to turn golden brown, shaking the pan to dissolve the sugar.

2 Add the blackberries to the pan and allow them to cook over high heat for 2–3 minutes, until they are heated through and softened, but have not broken up. Leave the berries to cool slightly while you toast the slices of brioche.

3 Thickly spread the mascarpone over the slices of toasted brioche and top with the sugary, fried berries. Spoon over any excess juice that is left in the pan and serve.

Late summer blackberries often usher in autumn puddings, like this crumble. One of the best soft fruits for freezing, blackberries can deliver a welcome blast of vitamin C in the colder months.

Blackberry
and apple crumble

Serves 6–8 • **Prep** 15–20 mins • **Cooking** 45 mins

INGREDIENTS

1kg (2¼lb) apples, peeled, cored, and thickly sliced
350g (12oz) blackberries
200g (7oz) dark muscovado sugar
125g (4½oz) butter, diced
125g (4½oz) plain flour
125g (4½oz) coarse oatmeal or porridge oats
double cream or custard, to serve

METHOD

1 Preheat the oven to 180°C (350°F/Gas 4). Put the apples in a wide, shallow, 2.25 litre (4 pint) ovenproof dish. Add the blackberries. Sprinkle about 3 tbsp of the sugar over the fruit. Cover with foil and pop in the oven for 15 minutes to soften the fruit.

2 Make the crumble by rubbing together the butter and flour until it resembles breadcrumbs. Add the remaining sugar and then the oats; you could do this in a blender, adding the oats last so they are not chopped too finely.

3 Remove the fruit from the oven, give it a quick stir, and spread the crumble all over. Cook in the oven for another 30 minutes or until the fruit is oozing out from beneath the golden crumble. Serve with double cream or custard.

In this wonderful cheesecake recipe, the blueberries are reduced to a thick purée and swirled into the creamy topping. Its marbled appearance makes it look exceptionally pretty.

Blueberry-ripple
cheesecake

Serves 8 • **Prep** 20 mins • **Cooking** 40 mins

INGREDIENTS

50g (1³/₄oz) butter, plus
    extra for greasing
125g (4¹/₂oz) digestive biscuits
150g (5¹/₂oz) blueberries
150g (5¹/₂oz) caster sugar,
    plus 3 tbsp extra
400g (14oz) cream cheese
250g (9oz) mascarpone cheese
2 large eggs, plus 1 large
    egg yolk
¹/₂ tsp natural vanilla extract
2 tbsp plain flour

METHOD

1 Preheat the oven to 180°C (350°F/Gas 4). Grease a 20cm (8in) loose-bottomed cake tin. Put the biscuits in a plastic bag and crush with a rolling pin. Melt the butter in a pan, then add the biscuit crumbs and stir until well-coated. Press the crumbs into the base of the tin.

2 Put the blueberries and 3 tablespoons of caster sugar in a food processor and whizz until smooth, then push the mixture through a sieve into a small pan. Bring to a boil, then allow to simmer for 3–5 minutes, or until thickened and jammy. Set aside.

3 Put all the remaining ingredients into the cleaned food processor and whizz until well combined. Pour the mixture onto the biscuit base and smooth the top. With a teaspoon, carefully drizzle the blueberry mixture over the cream cheese mixture in a swirly pattern. Bake the cheesecake for 40 minutes, or until it has set but still has a slight wobble in the middle when you shake the tin. Leave to cool in the oven for an hour, then remove from the oven and cool completely before serving.

BLUEBERRIES

When to pick
Pick blueberries when they are dark purple, with their blush starting to fade, and they are full of juice but still firm. If in doubt, try one to test for sweetness.

Eat and store fresh
Eat blueberries within 2 days of picking if using raw, or store in the fridge for up to 3 days if you are cooking them.

How to preserve
Blueberries can be made into jams and jellies. They can also be bottled or used in cordials and syrups.

Freezing options
Open freeze whole on trays, as a cooked or uncooked purée, as a freezer jam (see pages 176–7), or blanched or poached in sugar syrup (see pages 194–5).

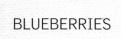

As long as you protect them from the birds, blueberries are easy to grow and prolific. Here, a classic American recipe is used to showcase one of the sweetest berries around.

Blueberry cobbler

Serves 4 • **Prep** 15 mins • **Cooking** 30 mins

INGREDIENTS

450g (1lb) blueberries
2 large peaches or 2 dessert
    apples, sliced
grated zest of $^1/_2$ lemon
2 tbsp caster sugar

For the cobbler
225g (8oz) self-raising flour
2 tsp baking powder
75g (2$^1/_2$oz) caster sugar, plus
    1 tbsp for sprinkling
pinch of salt
75g (2$^1/_2$oz) butter,
    chilled and diced
1 egg
100ml (3$^1/_2$fl oz) buttermilk
handful of flaked almonds

METHOD

1 Preheat the oven to 190°C (375°F/Gas 5). Spread the blueberries and peaches over the base of a shallow ovenproof dish and sprinkle with the lemon zest and sugar.

2 Sift the flour, baking powder, caster sugar, and salt into a bowl. Add the butter, and work with your fingers until the mixture resembles breadcrumbs.

3 Break the egg into the buttermilk and beat well. Add to the dry ingredients and mix together to form a soft, sticky dough. Drop walnut-sized spoonfuls of the mixture over the top of the fruit, leaving a little space between them. Press them down lightly with your fingers, then sprinkle over the flaked almonds and 1 tbsp of sugar.

4 Bake for 30 minutes, or until golden and bubbling, covering it loosely with kitchen foil if it is browning too quickly. It is done when a skewer pushed into the middle of the cobbler crust comes out clean. Leave to cool briefly before serving.

Making a simple jam like this is a great way of preserving your blueberries. It is undeniably sweet, and perfect on its own with natural yogurt or as an accompaniment to some warm scones.

Blueberry jam

Makes approx. 450g (1lb) or 2 small jars • **Prep** 5 mins • **Cooking** 35 mins

INGREDIENTS

900g (2lb) blueberries
juice of 2 lemons
675g (1½lb) caster or
    granulated sugar

METHOD

1 Put the blueberries, 150ml (5fl oz) of water, and the lemon juice into a preserving pan or a large heavy saucepan. Bring to a boil, then simmer for 10–15 minutes to extract the pectin and soften the fruit.

2 Add the sugar, stir until it dissolves, then increase the heat and bring the mixture to a boil. Boil rapidly for 10–12 minutes, or until it reaches the setting point. Take the pan off the heat while you test for a set (see pages 186–7).

3 With the pan still off the heat, use a large skimmer to skim any surface scum off the jam. Leave the jam to cool slightly, then ladle into warm sterilized jars, cover with discs of waxed paper, seal, and label.

Note Keeps for 6–9 months. Store in a cool, dark place and refrigerate after opening.

Freeze fruit

A perfect way to preserve the flavour and nutritional content of fruit is to freeze it, but only freeze fresh, top-quality crops. Freezing breaks down the cell walls of the fruit, so whole fruit will be squashy when thawed, but its flavour will be just as delicious as fresh. All fruits are best frozen with sugar to help retain their texture when thawed. Remove any stones and cut larger fruits (apart from citrus fruits) in half or slices before freezing. The periods listed in the chart opposite are the maximum freezer storage times.

1 Open freeze Discard any overripe or blemished berries. Lay them in a single layer on baking trays. Sprinkle liberally with caster sugar and put in the freezer.

2 Put into bags As soon as the fruit is frozen (after 1 hour or so), scrape it from the trays and put it into portion-sized freezer bags. Label, date, and return to freezer.

FREEZER TIMES FOR FRUITS

FRUITS	RAW			COOKED	
	Sprinkle with sugar and open freeze on trays (Months)	Pack in freezer pots, cover in syrup or sugar, and freeze (Months)	Purée, pack in freezer pots, and freeze (Months)	Blanch or poach in syrup, pack in freezer pots, cover in syrup, and freeze (Months)	Purée, pack in freezer pots, and freeze (Months)
Apples	9	9	—	9	9
Apricots (ripe)	9	9	6	9	9
Blackberries	12	12	6	9	9
Blackcurrants	12	12	6	9	9
Blueberries	12	12	6	9	9
Cherries	6	6	6	9	9
Cranberries	12	12	6	9	9
Figs	9	9	6	9	9
Gooseberries	12	12	6	9	9
Melons	9	9	6	9	9
Nectarines	9	9	6	9	9
Peaches	9	9	6	9	9
Pears	—	—	—	9	9
Plums (all kinds)	9	9	6	9	9
Raspberries	12	12	6	9	9
Rhubarb	12	12	—	9	9
Strawberries	9	9	6	9	9

How to freeze purées and cooked fruit

Very juicy fruits such as peaches, raspberries, or strawberries can be puréed uncooked in a food processor with a little sugar and lemon juice. Fruit not perfect enough to freeze uncooked can be stewed lightly, baked, or poached in a sugar syrup. Freeze purées for up to 6 months and cooked fruit for up to 9 months, leaving 2cm (³/₄in) of space at the top of each pot to allow for expansion.

Home-grown blackcurrants are one of the treats of the allotment and are often expensive to buy. Here, the delicate fragrance of rosemary enhances this sweet, sharp, and creamy dessert.

Blackcurrant
and rosemary cheesecake

Serves 8–10 • **Prep** 20 mins • **Cooking** 1–1 hour 15 mins, plus chilling

INGREDIENTS

For the cheesecake

85g (3oz) butter, plus extra
   for greasing
200g (7oz) digestive biscuits
1 tbsp chopped rosemary
675g (1½lb) cream cheese
225g (8oz) caster sugar
2 eggs
1 tsp natural vanilla extract

For the topping

225g (8oz) blackcurrants
caster sugar, to taste
1 tsp arrowroot

METHOD

1 Preheat the oven to 150°C (300°F/Gas 2). Grease a 20cm (8in) loose-bottomed cake tin. Put the biscuits in a plastic bag and crush with a rolling pin. Melt the butter in a pan, then add the biscuit crumbs and rosemary, and stir until well coated. Press the crumbs into the base of the tin.

2 Beat the cheese with the sugar, eggs, and vanilla extract. Spoon into the prepared tin. Level the surface. Bake for up to 1¼ hours, until set. Turn off the oven and leave until cold. Chill.

3 Stew the blackcurrants in 4 tbsp water until the juices run, but the currants still hold their shape. Sweeten to taste. Blend the arrowroot with 1 tsp water and stir in. Cook, stirring, until thickened and clear. Leave to cool.

4 Remove the cheesecake from the tin and place on a serving plate. Spoon the blackcurrant topping over so that the fruits trickle down the sides a little.

BLACKCURRANTS

When to pick
Blackcurrants mature for a few days after turning black, so pick when almost bursting but before they start to shrivel. They should be sweet but still sharp.

Eat and store fresh
Eat blackcurrants as soon as possible after picking if using them raw. If you are cooking them, they will keep for up to 3 days in the fridge.

How to preserve
A classic component of jams and jellies, they can also be bottled and used in both cordials and syrups.

Freezing options
Open freeze whole on trays, as a cooked or uncooked purée, as a freezer jam (see pages 176–7), or blanched or poached in sugar syrup (see pages 194–5).

A creamy, delicate dessert that works marvellously well with the sweet sharpness of the hot berry sauce. Use whatever fresh berries you have available, but make sure they are well sweetened.

Chilled rice pudding
with warm berry sauce

Serves 4–6 • **Prep** 10 mins • **Cooking** 20 mins

INGREDIENTS

For the rice pudding

800ml (1¼ pints) whole milk

150g (5½oz) long grain
   or basmati rice

50g (1¾oz) caster sugar

280ml (9fl oz) double cream

85g (3oz) blanched almonds,
   toasted and finely chopped

1 tbsp sweet sherry

1 tsp natural vanilla extract

For the sauce

300g (10½oz) mixed berries,
   such as blackcurrants,
   raspberries, and
   blackberries

50g (1¾oz) caster sugar

1 tbsp water

METHOD

1 Mix the milk, rice, and sugar in a large, heavy-bottomed pan and bring to a boil, stirring frequently to prevent the rice from sticking. Turn down the heat and simmer for 15 minutes or until the rice is soft, stirring frequently. Turn the rice out into a bowl and leave to cool.

2 While the rice cools, whip the cream until it rises in soft peaks, then fold it into the cooled rice.

3 Dry fry the almonds in a frying pan over low heat until golden. Leave to cool, and then chop. Fold the chopped almonds, sherry, and vanilla extract into the rice and leave in the fridge for 3–4 hours or overnight to chill before serving.

4 To make the sauce, heat the currants and berries gently with the sugar and water, and simmer on low heat for 3–4 minutes until they are cooked through. Purée the sauce with a hand-held blender and pass through a sieve. Pour the hot sauce over the chilled pudding to serve.

MELONS

When to pick
Pick melons when they start to smell fragrant. The area around the stalk starts to soften slightly and the stalk itself may start to crack. Ripe melons should also be heavy for their size, with unblemished skin.

Eat and store fresh
Eat all melons, except watermelon, at room temperature within a couple of days of picking. Store in a cool place for up to 5 days, depending on their ripeness. Watermelon is best served chilled.

How to preserve
Melons can be bottled or preserved in jams and pickles.

❄ **Freezing options**
Open freeze in slices on trays, as an uncooked or cooked purée, or slices blanched in sugar syrup (see pages 194–5).

Despite its unlikely combination of ingredients, this salad is fast becoming a modern classic. The sweetness of the ripe melon contrasts wonderfully with the salty feta and the heat of the chilli.

Watermelon salad with
feta and pumpkin seeds

Serves 4 • **Prep** 10 mins • **Cooking** 5 mins

INGREDIENTS

60g (2oz) pumpkin seeds
sea salt
1/4 tsp chilli powder
4 tbsp light olive oil
juice of 1 lemon
freshly ground black pepper
500g (1lb 2oz) watermelon, peeled, deseeded if preferred, and diced into 2cm (3/4in) squares
1/2 red onion, peeled and finely sliced
4 large handfuls of mixed salad leaves, such as watercress, rocket, or baby spinach
300g (101/2oz) feta cheese, diced into 1cm (1/2in) squares

METHOD

1 Dry fry the pumpkin seeds for 2–3 minutes, until they start to pop. Add a pinch of salt and the chilli powder, stir, and cook for another minute. Set aside to cool.

2 In a large bowl whisk together the olive oil, lemon juice, and salt and pepper to taste. Add the watermelon, red onion, and salad leaves, and toss well to coat with the dressing.

3 Scatter the feta cheese and the seeds over the top of the salad and serve immediately.

This decidedly grown-up dessert is quick to prepare and visually appealing. Use only the ripest, most fragrant melons. For the best flavour, serve chilled rather than cold.

Melon slices
with vodka and orange

Serves 6–8 • **Prep** 5 mins, plus 15 mins marinating

INGREDIENTS

1 honeydew melon, cut in
    quarters lengthways,
    rind and seeds removed,
    and flesh sliced
1 watermelon, cut in half,
    rind and seeds removed,
    and flesh sliced
1–2 tbsp good-quality vodka
1–2 tbsp fresh orange juice,
    without bits
handful of mint leaves,
    roughly torn

METHOD

1 Arrange the melon slices in a large flat serving bowl or platter, drizzle with the vodka and orange juice, then leave to sit for 15 minutes while the fruit absorbs the juices.

2 Sprinkle with the mint and serve.

Note You can use any kind of melon, but always try to include watermelon, which will absorb the vodka.

A clafoutis is rather like a pastryless tart, where the cream, sugar, and eggs, are combined to make a rich batter. This French dessert is a fantastic way to use up a glut of cherries.

Cherry clafoutis

Serves 6 • **Prep** 12 mins, plus standing • **Cooking** 35–45 mins

INGREDIENTS

750g (1lb 10oz) cherries, destoned

3 tbsp kirsch

75g (2¹⁄₂oz) caster sugar

butter, for greasing

4 large eggs

1 vanilla pod, split

100g (3¹⁄₂oz) plain flour, sifted

300ml (10fl oz) milk

pinch of salt

icing sugar, to serve

METHOD

1 Toss the cherries with the kirsch and 2 tbsp of the sugar in a medium-sized bowl, and leave to stand for 30 minutes.

2 Meanwhile, preheat the oven to 200°C (400°F/Gas 6). Butter a 25cm (10in) flan tin, and set aside.

3 Strain the liquid from the cherries and beat it with the eggs, the seeds from the vanilla pod, and the remaining sugar. Slowly beat in the flour, then add the milk and salt, and mix to make a smooth batter.

4 Arrange the cherries in the dish, then pour over the batter. Place in the oven and bake for 35–45 minutes, or until the top is browned and the centre is firm to the touch.

5 Leave to cool slightly, then serve warm, dusted with icing sugar. Clafoutis is also good at room temperature.

Variation You can substitute damsons or other small plums for the cherries, adding more sugar if necessary, to compensate for the extra tartness.

This luscious jam has just a hint of brandy in it to cut through the sweetness of the cherries. A cherry pitter is a useful device, but if you don't have one halve the cherries and remove the stones.

Cherry jam

Makes approx. 1kg (2¼lb) or 3 medium jars • **Prep** 20 mins • **Cooking** 30–35 mins

INGREDIENTS

500g (1lb 2oz) dark cherries, pitted, with the stones reserved

juice of 2 lemons

500g (1lb 2oz) caster or granulated sugar, plus added pectin as per manufacturer's instructions, or 500g (1lb 2oz) jam sugar

2 tbsp brandy or cherry brandy

METHOD

1 Place the cherry stones in a small square of muslin, gather into a bag, and tie with string. Put the cherries in a preserving pan or a large heavy saucepan, with the bag of cherry stones, and pour in 300ml (10fl oz) of water. Bring to a boil, then reduce to a simmer and cook for 10–15 minutes or until the cherries are tender and are beginning to soften. Discard the stones. If you want some of the cherries to remain chunky in the jam, don't cook them for too long.

2 Pour in the lemon juice, and add either the sugar and pectin, or the jam sugar. Heat gently, stirring until all the sugar has dissolved. Bring to a boil and keep at a steady rolling boil, stirring occasionally, for about 10 minutes or until the jam reaches setting point. Remove the pan from the heat while you test for a set (see pages 186–7).

3 Stir in the brandy, then ladle into warm sterilized jars, cover with discs of waxed paper, seal, and label.

Note Keeps for 9 months. Store in a cool, dark place, and refrigerate after opening.

Bottle fruit in alcohol

Many fruits bottle well in alcohol and make a luxurious treat that will taste better than anything available to buy. You will be spoilt for choice when deciding which seasonal fruits to treat in this way. Fruits preserved in brandy, rum, whisky, vodka, gin, or eau de vie taste deliciously boozy. Serve with coffee, add to ice creams and other desserts along with the fragrant liquor, or use the fruits in cakes. This method particularly suits juicy, thin-skinned berries, plums, and cherries. Once bottled, store in a cool, dark place for 2–3 months to mature before opening.

1 **Put cherries in jars** Carefully place the cherries in some wide-necked, sterilized preserving jars, packing them in tightly while taking care not to squash or bruise them.

2 **Fill with alcohol** Add enough sugar to fill one-third of the jar and top with brandy. (As a general guide, use $^1/_4$–$^1/_3$ sugar and $^3/_4$–$^2/_3$ alcohol to fruit.)

Recipe Cherries in brandy

Makes approx. 750ml (1¼ pints) or 3 small preserving jars • **Prep** 10 mins • **Keeps** 12 months or longer

INGREDIENTS

500g (1lb 2oz) just-ripe cherries (sweet or Morello) in perfect condition, washed and de-stalked

approx. 175g (6oz) caster sugar
approx. 350ml (12fl oz) brandy

Other fruits to preserve in alcohol

Almost all fruits bottle well in alcohol, some exceptions being apples, melons, and rhubarb.

Blackberries Preserve in gin, vodka, or brandy.
Clementines Remove pith and preserve in vodka.
Nectarines and peaches Use sun-ripened, freshly-picked fruit, destone, and bottle in rum.
Pears Bottle in brandy or eau de vie.
Raspberries A classic fruit to add to a rumtopf, or to make liqueurs and cordials.
Plums Good in brandy with a cinnamon stick or star anise.

3 **Dissolve sugar** Tap the jar gently on a board and turn it to release air bubbles, and seal. Occasionally shake or turn the jar upside down to help the sugar dissolve.

4 **Leave to mature** Store in a cool, dark place for 2–3 months to allow the flavours to fully mature before opening. Refrigerate after opening.

PEACHES

When to pick
Pick peaches when they come away from the tree easily. They should give slightly if squeezed, and often have a pinkish blush and a sweet fragrance when ripe.

Eat and store fresh
Eat when slightly soft, at room temperature. Depending on when they are picked, they will keep for up to 5 days at room temperature.

How to preserve
Peaches can be sliced and dried, as well as used in all kinds of jams and jellies, savoury chutneys, and preserves. They have a low pectin content, so crack the stones open and use the kernels to help setting, as with apricots.

Freezing options
Destone, slice, and open freeze on trays, as a cooked or uncooked purée, as a freezer jam (see pages 176–7), or blanched or poached in sugar syrup (see pages 194–5).

The classic peach melba is a delightful combination of vanilla ice cream, fresh peaches, and a raspberry sauce. The three flavours marry to make a deliciously delicate and fragrant ice cream.

Peach melba ice cream

Serves 4–6 • Prep 30 mins, plus churning and freezing • Cooking 15 mins

INGREDIENTS

300ml (10fl oz) double cream
300ml (10fl oz) whole milk
3 large egg yolks
1 tsp natural vanilla extract
150g (5½oz) caster sugar
100g (3½oz) fresh raspberries
4 ripe peaches, destoned, peeled, and diced

METHOD

1 Heat the cream and milk gently in a saucepan until it almost boils, then take off the heat. In another bowl, whisk together the egg yolks, vanilla extract, and 100g (3½oz) of sugar until fluffy. Pour the cream and milk over the egg mixture, whisking continuously. Return the mixture to the cleaned pan. Bring to a boil, reduce the heat, and simmer for 6–8 minutes, stirring continuously, until the custard thickens. Transfer the mixture to a bowl and leave it to cool, stirring occasionally, to prevent skin forming, or cover the surface with greaseproof paper for the same reason.

2 Put the raspberries and 25g (1oz) of sugar in a bowl, blend, pass through a sieve and pour into a jug. Blend the peaches and 25g (1oz) of sugar and pour into another jug.

3 When cold, process the custard in an ice cream maker for 20–30 minutes until nearly frozen. Add the peach purée and process for another 10–15 minutes to a frozen consistency. Transfer to a plastic container and drizzle the raspberry purée over. Use a skewer to draw the purée through the ice cream to make a ripple effect. Freeze for a few hours before eating.

This rich, chunky preserve is just as delicious spooned over ice cream as it is spread on freshly baked bread. Use only the ripest peaches in this sumptuous recipe.

Peach and walnut
preserve

Makes approx. 1kg (2¹/₄lb) or 3 medium jars • **Prep** 25 mins • **Cooking** 20–25 mins

INGREDIENTS

1.25kg (2³/₄lb) ripe peaches

1 orange, peeled but with pith still attached, finely sliced

900g (2lb) caster or granulated sugar

juice of 1 lemon

50g (1³/₄oz) walnuts, roughly chopped

1–2 tbsp brandy (optional)

METHOD

1 Cut a cross in the peach skins and plunge them in boiling water for 30 seconds. Plunge in cold water and peel away the skins. Cut them in half, remove the stones and reserve them, and chop the flesh. Layer the peaches and orange slices in a large bowl with the sugar, cover, and leave for at least 4 hours or overnight.

2 Tip the fruit and sugar into a preserving pan or a large heavy saucepan. Place the peach stones in a small square of muslin, gather into a small bag, tie with string, and add it to the pan. Cook over gentle heat, stirring until the sugar dissolves. Bring to a boil and cook at a rolling boil for 15–20 minutes or until set. Remove the pan from the heat while you test for a set (see pages 186–7).

3 Remove the muslin bag of peach stones, then stir in the lemon juice, walnuts, and brandy (if using). Ladle into warm sterilized jars, cover with discs of waxed paper, seal, and label.

Note Store in a cool, dark place, and refrigerate after opening. Keeps for 6 months.

Here ripe peaches are surrounded with a delicate frangipane to produce a classic French fruit tart that would work equally well made with summer berries, apricots, plums, or nectarines.

Almond and peach frangipane

Serves 8 • **Prep** 20 mins • **Cooking** 30 mins

INGREDIENTS

250g (9oz) ready-made
    shortcrust pastry
100g (3^1/$_2$oz) butter, at
    room temperature
100g (3^1/$_2$oz) caster sugar
2 large eggs
100g (3^1/$_2$oz) ground almonds
25g (scant 1oz) plain flour,
    plus extra to dust
4 peaches, halved and destoned
icing sugar, to dust for serving

METHOD

1 Preheat the oven to 200°C (400°F/Gas 6). Put a baking tray in the oven to heat up. On a surface lightly dusted with flour, roll out the pastry to a thickness of about 5mm (^{1}/$_4$in), and line a rectangular baking tin measuring 12 x 36cm (5 x 14^1/$_2$in). Trim off the excess pastry with a knife and set the tart case to one side while you make the filling.

2 Place the butter and sugar in a bowl and whisk with an electric hand whisk until creamy, then beat in the eggs. Mix in the ground almonds and flour until well combined, then smooth the mixture into the pastry case. Press the peach halves cut-side down into the almond mixture.

3 Sit the tin on the hot baking tray, then bake for 30 minutes or until the almond mixture is golden brown and cooked through. Dust with icing sugar before serving warm or cold.

Pork works beautifully with soft fruits like apricots. The addition of cream and whisky turns this speedy supper into something truly special. Wonderful served with mashed potato.

Caramelized pork
with pecans and apricots

Serves 4 • **Prep** 10 mins • **Cooking** 15 mins

INGREDIENTS

1–2 tsp light soft brown sugar

675g (1½lb) pork tenderloin
    (in one piece)

1 tbsp extra virgin olive oil

knob of butter

handful of pecan nuts

handful of apricots, halved
    and destoned

splash of whisky (optional)

300ml (10fl oz) double cream

METHOD

1 Rub the brown sugar over the pork, then slice the pork horizontally into thick medallions.

2 Heat the oil and butter in a frying pan over medium–high heat. Brown the pork medallions for 3–4 minutes on each side until golden. Remove the pork from the pan and add the pecan nuts, browning them in the hot oil for 2 minutes. Return the pork to the pan and add the apricot halves.

3 Increase the heat to high and add the whisky (if using). Let it simmer for 2 minutes until the alcohol has evaporated. Reduce the heat to medium, pour over the cream and let it simmer for 2–3 minutes more, making sure that the apricots are tender but not collapsing.

Note If you don't have fresh apricots use dried instead.

APRICOTS

When to pick
Pick apricots when they have a deep colour and a sweet fragrance. They should come away easily from the branch. Do not allow them to become too soft.

Eat and store fresh
Keep at room temperature and eat within 2–3 days of harvesting if eating raw. If cooking, they can be kept for 3–5 days in the fridge.

How to preserve
Apricots make delicious jams (see page 219) and jellies. Their low pectin content can be offset by adding some of the kernels, cracked and wrapped in muslin, to the pan to aid setting.

Freezing options
Destone, slice, and open freeze on trays, as a cooked or uncooked purée, as a freezer jam (see pages 176–7), or blanched or poached in sugar syrup (see pages 194–5).

Make conserves

Conserves differ from jams in that they contain large pieces of fruit or whole fruits and can be made with less sugar. The fruits are steeped in sugar before cooking to firm them up, and they are boiled more gently than jam. They can be used in different ways, such as glazes for fruit tarts and flans, as cake fillings, or on yogurt. They can also be served like jam with bread. The best fruits for making conserves include apricots, blackberries, greengages, dessert plums, strawberries, cherries, and nectarines.

1 Layer the apricots and sugar Wash, halve, and destone the apricots. Layer them with the sugar in a bowl, cover, and leave for 2–3 hours or overnight at room temperature.

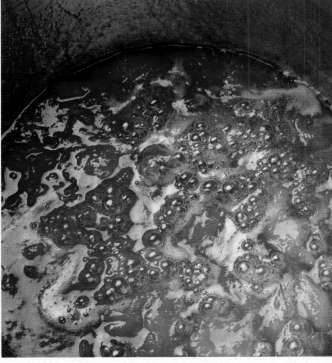

2 Bring to a boil Put the fruit and sugar in a preserving pan with the lemon juice. Heat gently, stir. Do not break up the fruit. Bring to a steady boil for 7–10 minutes.

Recipe Apricot conserve

Makes 700g (1½lb) or 2 medium jars • **Prep** 25–30 mins, plus standing • **Keeps** 6 months

INGREDIENTS

500g (1lb 2oz) ripe apricots

350g (12oz) caster or
    granulated sugar

juice of 1 lemon

Tips on making conserves

Adapt the basic conserve recipe shown here in the following ways for slightly different results.

Use less sugar For a fresher flavour.

Make a luxurious conserve Add a small glass of wine at the same time as the sugar, or a splash of liqueur or spirit just before potting.

Keep the fruit intact Try not to stir once the sugar has dissolved. Set juicy fruit aside in step 2. Boil the sugar and juices until reduced. Add the fruit and complete the boiling process.

3 Test for a set Take the pan off the heat, test for a set with a cold saucer (see page 187), then leave to cool until it has formed a wrinkle on the surface.

4 Pot up and store Ladle into clean, hot, sterilized jars, ensuring an even amount of juice and fruit per jar. Cover with waxed paper, seal, label, and store in a cool, dark place.

AUTUMN

Pumpkins
and squashes

Onions

Shallots

Garlic

Kohl rabi

Celery

Beetroots

Carrots

Sweet
potatoes

Cranberries

Grapes

Apples

Pears

Quinces

Plums

Figs

When to pick

Pick summer squashes often. Leave pumpkins and winter squashes until the foliage is dying back, harvest with 10cm (4in) of stalk, and leave them in the sun for 1 week to cure (see page 263).

Eat and store fresh

Store summer squashes for up to 5 days in the fridge. Winter squashes and pumpkins keep for up to 6 months in a cool, dark place.

How to preserve

Both varieties can be used in chutneys, pickles, and relishes.

Freezing options

Slice, blanch briefly, cool, and freeze summer squashes for up to 6 months. Cut pumpkins and winter squashes into chunks and freeze raw for up to 6 months.

In this delicious autumn soup, the natural sweetness of the pumpkin is offset by sharp apples. Garnishing the finished soup with toasted pumpkin seeds adds a welcome crunch.

Pumpkin
and apple soup

Serves 6 • **Prep** 20 mins • **Cooking** 40 mins

INGREDIENTS

60g (2oz) unsalted butter

1 medium onion, finely chopped

200g (7oz) pumpkin, peeled, seeds removed, and diced

2 sharp-tasting apples such as Granny Smith, diced

1.2 litres (2 pints) cold vegetable stock or chicken stock

sea salt and freshly ground black pepper

30g (1oz) toasted pumpkin seeds, to garnish

METHOD

1 Melt the butter in a large saucepan, add the onion, and cook very gently, stirring often, for 10 minutes or until soft. Do not let it brown. Add the pumpkin and apples and stir to coat well. Pour in 150ml (5fl oz) hot water, cover with a lid, and leave on very low heat for 30 minutes, stirring from time to time. If the liquid evaporates, pour in a little more hot water. The vegetables and fruit should be very soft at the end of cooking.

2 Meanwhile, toast the pumpkin seeds in a dry frying pan over medium heat, until browned but not burnt.

3 Stir in the stock, then blend the soup with a hand-held blender or in batches in a food processor. Pour the blended soup through a sieve, set over a clean saucepan. Press the contents through with the back of a ladle, a wooden spoon, or a pestle.

4 When all the soup has been sieved, reheat it very gently, then season to taste with salt and pepper. Serve garnished with the toasted pumpkin seeds.

Here a punchy combination of mint, lime, chilli, and ginger enhances the sweetness of the squash. This is a fantastic side dish for roast beef or chicken.

Roasted squash
with ginger

Serves 3–4 • **Prep** 20 mins • **Cooking** 40 mins

INGREDIENTS

1 butternut squash, peeled,
   seeds removed and sliced
   into big, thick strips
5 tbsp extra virgin olive oil
1 tsp salt
2 red chillies, deseeded
   and finely chopped
60g (2oz) root ginger, grated
   or finely sliced
1 tbsp clear honey
freshly ground black pepper
handful of mint leaves, torn
2 limes, cut into wedges

METHOD

1 Preheat the oven to 180°C (350°F/Gas 4). Place the slices of squash in a roasting tin. Mix together 2 tbsp warm water, the olive oil, salt, chillies, ginger, honey, and pepper to taste. Drizzle the sauce over the squash, mixing to coat well.

2 Bake the squash for 40 minutes, or until tender, shaking occasionally during cooking to avoid sticking. If the squash dries out, add a little more olive oil.

3 Transfer the warm squash to a large serving dish, and scatter with the mint. Serve with lime wedges to squeeze over.

This spicy dip vivid orange dip can be served slightly chunky, or processed until smooth. Try it served on grilled sourdough bread with grilled pancetta on top.

Roasted pumpkin
and ginger dip

Serves 8 • **Prep** 20 mins • **Cooking** 30 mins

INGREDIENTS

1kg (2¼lb) pumpkin, peeled, seeds removed, and cut into chunks

4 tbsp extra virgin olive oil, plus extra for drizzling (optional)

4 whole garlic cloves, crushed with the back of a knife

1 tbsp grated or finely chopped root ginger

sea salt and freshly ground black pepper

1 medium-hot, long red chilli, deseeded and sliced

4 sprigs of flat-leaf parsley, leaves only

grated zest and juice of 1 lemon

150ml (5fl oz) Greek-style yogurt

pinch of paprika

METHOD

1 Preheat the oven to 200°C (400°F/Gas 6). Put the pumpkin on a baking tray, and toss with the olive oil, garlic, and ginger. Season with salt and black pepper. Roast for about 30 minutes until tender and golden. Remove from the oven and leave to cool.

2 Transfer the cooled pumpkin to a blender or food processor, and add the chilli, parsley (reserving a little to garnish), and lemon zest and juice. Blend to a chunky or smooth purée, depending on taste.

3 Put the pumpkin purée and the yogurt in a bowl, and mix thoroughly. Season if needed, then spoon into a serving bowl. Top with a drizzle of extra virgin olive oil (if using). Garnish with the reserved parsley and paprika.

Variation The recipe works equally well with butternut squash.

Ripening pumpkins and squashes herald the onset of autumn. This pasta dish is perfect for those slightly cooler days, as it has the comfort of cream and the warmth of red chillies.

Butternut squash pasta
in chilli and Parmesan sauce

Serves 4 • **Prep** 20 mins • **Cooking** 30 mins

INGREDIENTS

200g (7oz) butternut squash, peeled and diced

1–2 tbsp extra virgin olive oil

sea salt and freshly ground black pepper

1 garlic clove, crushed

1/2 red chilli, deseeded and finely chopped

8 sage leaves

150ml (5fl oz) single cream

25g (scant 1oz) Parmesan cheese, grated, plus extra to finish

350g (12oz) conchiglie pasta

METHOD

1 Preheat the oven to 200°C/400°F/Gas 6. Toss the squash in a little olive oil, season it well with salt and pepper, and roast for 30 minutes or until soft. Remove it from the oven and leave to cool for a few minutes.

2 Meanwhile, gently fry the garlic, chilli, and sage in a little olive oil for 2–3 minutes.

3 Once the butternut squash has cooled slightly, put it into a blender or food processor. Add the cream, Parmesan, garlic, chilli, sage leaves, plenty of black pepper, and a little salt. Blend it all to a fine purée, adding 1–2 tablespoons of water if it looks too thick.

4 Cook the pasta until al dente and drain it. Quickly reheat the sauce in the pasta pan, adding more water if it seems a little stiff. Put the pasta back into the pan and mix it well, allowing the sauce to coat the pasta. Serve with plenty of fresh Parmesan to finish.

Most squashes ripen once the summer is drawing to a close and the cook's thoughts naturally turn towards autumnal fare. This spicy tagine fits the bill, using the best of the early-autumn produce.

Butternut squash tagine

Serves 4 • **Prep** 20 mins • **Cooking** 1 hour

INGREDIENTS

4 tbsp light olive oil

2 red onions, finely chopped

1 large red pepper, deseeded,
    trimmed, and diced

4 garlic cloves, chopped

1 thumb-sized piece
    ginger, finely chopped

1 tsp chilli powder

1 tsp cinnamon

2 tsp smoked paprika

2 tsp ground coriander

1 tbsp ground cumin

2 x 400g cans chopped
    tomatoes

700ml (1 pint) vegetable stock

2 tbsp clear honey

sea salt and freshly ground
    black pepper

400g (14oz) butternut squash,
    peeled, deseeded, and diced

200g (7oz) cooked chickpeas

100g (3½oz) dried apricots

bunch of coriander leaves

METHOD

1 Pour the olive oil into a large saucepan. Add the onions, red pepper, garlic, and ginger, and fry over low heat for 2 minutes until softened, but not brown.

2 Add the chilli, cinnamon, smoked paprika, ground coriander, and cumin, and continue to cook for another 2 minutes over low heat, to release the flavour of the spices. Add the tomatoes, stock, and honey, and season well. Bring the sauce to a boil and turn down the heat. Simmer slowly, uncovered, for 30 minutes.

3 Add the butternut squash, chickpeas, and chopped dried apricots and continue to cook for 10–15 minutes until the squash is soft, but not falling apart. Add more water if it is beginning to look a little dry. Season to taste and stir in the chopped coriander before serving with some herby couscous.

Note Canned chickpeas can be used here, although dried ones that have been soaked overnight, then cooked until soft, give a better final texture.

Make this wonderful vegetarian tart in the early autumn when spinach and squash are readily available on the allotment. If you grow chard you can use it in place of the spinach.

Roasted squash
and Gorgonzola tart

Serves 6 • **Prep** 25 mins, plus chilling • **Cooking** 1 ½ hours

INGREDIENTS

250g (9oz) ready-made
    shortcrust pastry
450g (1lb) squash, peeled,
    seeds removed, thickly
    sliced
1–2 tbsp extra virgin olive oil
400g (14oz) spinach
2 large eggs
1 egg yolk
300ml (10fl oz) double cream
50g (1³/₄oz) Parmesan
    cheese, grated
pinch of freshly grated nutmeg
salt and freshly ground
    black pepper
115g (4oz) Gorgonzola
    cheese, crumbled

METHOD

1 Preheat the oven to 180°C (350°F/Gas 4). On a surface lightly dusted with flour, roll out the pastry to a thickness of about 3mm (¹/₈in) in a circle a little larger than a 20cm (8in) loose-bottomed tart tin. Line the tart tin with the pastry. Chill for 30 minutes.

2 Put the squash slices on a roasting tray and brush with olive oil. Bake for 30 minutes, or until tender. Meanwhile, place the spinach and a little olive oil in a saucepan and cook over medium heat for 4 minutes until wilted. Drain and leave to cool. Whisk the eggs, egg yolk, cream, Parmesan, and nutmeg together, and season to taste.

3 Line the pastry case with greaseproof paper, and fill with baking beans. Bake blind for 15 minutes. Remove the beans and paper, and bake for another 10 minutes.

4 Squeeze the spinach dry and spread it across the bottom of the tart case, then add the squash and Gorgonzola. Pour the egg mixture over and bake for 30–40 minutes, or until the filling is set. Remove from the oven and leave it to sit for 10 minutes before serving.

A selection of vegetables is simmered in Indian spices and vinegar to give this colourful chutney its flavour. If you like a hotter chutney, add one or two finely chopped green chillies.

Indian-spiced
vegetable chutney

Makes approx. 1.5kg (3lb 3oz) or 3 large jars • **Prep** 30 mins • **Cooking** 2–2 1/4 hours

INGREDIENTS

900g (2lb) butternut squash, seeds removed, peeled, and cut into bite-sized chunks

2 onions, finely chopped

225g (8oz) cooking apples, peeled, cored, and chopped

3 courgettes, halved lengthways and chopped

50g (1³/₄oz) ready-to-eat stoned dates, chopped

450ml (15fl oz) cider vinegar

2 tbsp medium or hot curry powder

1 tsp ground cumin

2.5cm (1in) piece of root ginger, grated or finely chopped

450g (1lb) granulated or light soft brown sugar

METHOD

1 Put the squash, onions, cooking apples, courgettes, and dates in a preserving pan or a large heavy, stainless steel saucepan. Pour over the vinegar, add the spices, and ginger, and mix well.

2 Bring the mixture to a boil, then reduce the heat and simmer for 40–45 minutes or until the vegetables are soft, stirring occasionally.

3 Add the sugar, stir until it has dissolved, then continue to cook on a gentle simmer for 1–1¹/₂ hours or until the chutney is thick and the liquid has been absorbed. Stir continuously near the end of the cooking time so that the chutney doesn't catch on the base of the pan.

4 Ladle into warm sterilized jars with non-metallic or vinegar-proof lids, making sure there are no air gaps. Cover each pot with a waxed paper disc, seal, and label.

Note Keeps for 12 months. Store in a cool, dark place. Allow the flavours to mature for at least 1 month, and refrigerate after opening.

This subtly spiced jam is superb served with strong blue cheese, or as a sweet jam spread on toast or bread. Choose smaller pumpkins with smooth flesh and a good flavour.

Pumpkin and orange
spiced jam

Makes approx. 2kg (4$\frac{1}{2}$lb) or 4 large jars • **Prep** 15 mins • **Cooking** 35–45 mins

INGREDIENTS

1.35kg (3lb) pumpkin, peeled, deseeded, and cut into small pieces

2 cooking apples, peeled, and chopped into small pieces

1.35kg (3lb) caster or granulated sugar

juice of 1 lemon

juice of 1 orange

pinch of cinnamon

pinch of freshly grated nutmeg

METHOD

1 Put the pumpkin and apple in a preserving pan or a large heavy saucepan. Pour in 50ml (2fl oz) of water (just enough to stop the pumpkin from catching and burning). Bring to a boil, then reduce to a simmer and cook for 10–20 minutes or until the pumpkin is soft. Mash roughly with a potato masher or fork, keeping a few chunks of pumpkin whole.

2 Add the sugar, lemon and orange juice, cinnamon, and nutmeg. Stir until all the sugar has dissolved. Then turn the heat up and bring to a boil. Cook at a rolling boil for 15–20 minutes or until the jam thickens and reaches the setting point. Remove the pan from the heat while you test for a set (see pages 186–7).

3 Ladle into warm sterilized jars, cover with waxed paper discs, seal, and label.

Note Store in a cool, dark place, and refrigerate after opening. Keeps for 6 months.

ONIONS

When to pick
Harvest onions when they reach a good size and the leaves begin to yellow. Leave to dry in the sun for 2 weeks to allow the skins to harden before storing.

Eat and store fresh
Milder red onions can be eaten raw in salads. All onions should be dried off and stored in a cool, dark place for 2–3 months (see pages 248–9).

How to preserve
A vital ingredient in pickles, relishes, and chutneys, onions can also star in recipes such as red onion marmalade (see page 241).

This timeless, warming soup is one of the best ways to use onions through the winter months. The brandy is optional, but the crispy croûtes oozing with melting Gruyère are not!

French onion soup

Serves 4 • **Prep** 10 mins • **Cooking** 1 hour 20 mins

INGREDIENTS

30g (1oz) butter

1 tbsp sunflower oil

675g (1½lb) onions, thinly sliced

1 tsp light soft brown sugar

sea salt and freshly ground black pepper

120ml (4fl oz) red wine

2 tbsp plain flour

1.5 litres (2¾ pints) hot beef stock

1 day-old baguette, cut into 1cm (½in) slices

4 tbsp brandy

1 garlic clove, cut in half

115g (4oz) Gruyère cheese or Emmental cheese, grated

METHOD

1 Melt the butter with the oil in a large, heavy pan over low heat. Add the onions and sugar, and turn to coat well. Season, then press a piece of damp greaseproof paper on top of the onions. Cook, uncovered, stirring occasionally for 40 minutes or until they are a rich, dark brown colour. Take care not to let them stick and burn.

2 Remove the greaseproof paper and stir in the wine. Increase the heat to medium and stir for 5 minutes while the onions glaze. Sprinkle in the flour, stir for 2 minutes, then pour in the stock and bring to a boil. Reduce the heat to low, cover, and simmer for 30 minutes. Taste and season with salt and pepper, if necessary.

3 To make the croûtes, toast 4 slices of the bread until golden. Alternatively, place on a baking sheet and bake in an oven preheated to 180°C (350°F/Gas 4) for 15 minutes.

4 Preheat the grill to its highest setting. Divide the soup among 4 flameproof bowls and stir 1 tbsp of the brandy into each. Rub the croûtes with cut garlic and place 1 in each bowl. Sprinkle the croûtes with the cheese and grill for 2–3 minutes or until the cheese is bubbling and golden.

The saltiness of the anchovies gives a welcome piquancy to this mild onion tart, which can be prepared a day in advance and reheated. Serve with a green salad.

Onion and anchovy tart

Serves 4–6 • **Prep** 15 mins, plus chilling • **Cooking** 1 1/4 hours

INGREDIENTS

250g (9oz) ready-made
　　shortcrust pastry
2 tbsp extra virgin olive oil
30g (1oz) butter
450g (1lb) onions, thinly sliced
750g (1lb 10oz) curd cheese
115ml (4fl oz) milk
2 large eggs
1 tsp cumin seeds or caraway
　　seeds, crushed (optional)
sea salt and freshly ground
　　black pepper
60g (2oz) anchovy fillets,
　　halved lengthways

METHOD

1 On a surface lightly dusted with flour, roll out the pastry to a thickness of about 3mm (1/8in) in a circle a little larger than a 20cm (8in) loose-bottomed tart tin. Line the tart tin with the pastry. Chill for 30 minutes.

2 Heat the oil and butter in a pan, and add the onions. Cover and cook over gentle heat, stirring occasionally, for 20 minutes, or until the onions are soft but not browned. Uncover and cook for a further 4–5 minutes, or until golden. Set aside to cool.

3 Preheat the oven to 200°C (400°F/Gas 6). Remove the tin from the fridge, line the pastry case with greaseproof paper, and fill with baking beans. Bake blind for 15 minutes. Remove the beans and paper, and bake for another 10 minutes.

4 Reduce the oven temperature to 180°C (350°F/Gas 4). Spoon the onions into the pastry case, spreading them in an even layer. Beat together the curd cheese, milk, eggs, and spices, if using. Season to taste with salt and pepper, then pour into the pastry case. Lay the anchovy fillets in a lattice pattern on top, and bake for 25 minutes, or until the pastry is golden and the filling is set. Serve warm.

This delicious marmalade made with sweet, sticky onions has now become a modern classic. Perfect served with cold meats and cheese.

Red onion marmalade

Makes approx. 700g (1½lb) or 2 medium jars • **Prep** 20 mins • **Cooking** 1 hour 10 mins

INGREDIENTS

2 tbsp extra virgin olive oil

1kg (2¼lb) red onions (approx. 6), peeled, halved, and sliced

sea salt and freshly ground black pepper

150ml (5fl oz) red wine

3 tbsp balsamic vinegar

3 tbsp white wine vinegar

6 tbsp light soft brown sugar

METHOD

1 Heat the oil in a preserving pan or a large heavy, stainless steel saucepan. Add the onions, a pinch of salt, and some pepper. Cook over low to medium heat for about 30 minutes until the onions soften and turn translucent, stirring occasionally so they don't catch and burn. Slow cooking is essential at this point, as this is where the delicious caramel taste is developed.

2 Raise the heat a little, add the wine and vinegars, and stir to combine. Bring to a boil, then reduce the heat, stir in the sugar, and cook on low heat, stirring occasionally, for another 30–40 minutes until most of the liquid has evaporated.

3 Remove the pan from the heat. Taste and adjust the seasoning as necessary, although the flavours will mature with time. Spoon into warm sterilized jars with non-metallic or vinegar-proof lids, making sure there are no air gaps. Cover with waxed paper discs, seal, and label. Store in a cool, dark place for at least 1 month to allow the flavours to develop.

Note Keeps for 3 months. Refrigerate after opening.

These crispy little fritters are made with gram flour, which can be found in most supermarkets. Try them served with a simple raita made of Greek yogurt, crushed garlic, and chopped mint.

Onion bhajis

Serves 4 • **Prep** 15 mins • **Cooking** 15 mins

INGREDIENTS

225g (8oz) onions, chopped

115g (4oz) gram (besan) flour

2 tsp cumin seeds

$^{1}/_{2}$ tsp turmeric

1 tsp ground coriander

1 green chilli or red chilli,
    deseeded, and very
    finely chopped

vegetable oil, for frying

METHOD

1 In a large bowl, mix together the onions, gram flour, cumin seeds, turmeric, coriander, and chilli. Add enough cold water (about 8 tbsp) to bind the mixture together to make a thick batter.

2 Half fill a deep saucepan or deep-fat fryer with oil and heat to 190°C (375°F). When hot, carefully place spoonfuls of the mixture, roughly the size of golf balls, into the oil, turning occasionally, until all sides are golden.

3 Remove the bhajis from the oil using a slotted spoon, and drain on kitchen paper.

4 Return the bhajis to the pan and quickly fry a second time until crisp and golden brown all over. Drain on kitchen paper and serve hot. The bhajis can be cooked up to the end of step 3 up to 4 hours in advance, and then given their second frying just before serving.

Variation To make vegetable bhajis, replace one-third of the onion with shredded spinach or grated carrot.

These smaller members of the allium family make a mild, sweet pickle using rich balsamic vinegar. Pour boiling water over the shallots for a few minutes and then drain, for easier peeling.

Pickled sweet shallots

Makes approx. 500g (1lb 2oz) • **Prep** 10 mins • **Cooking** 30–35 mins

INGREDIENTS

550g (1¼lb) shallots, peeled
a few sprigs of thyme
1 tbsp extra virgin olive oil
175ml (6fl oz) balsamic vinegar,
    plus extra if needed

METHOD

1 Preheat the oven to 200°C (400°F/Gas 6). Put the shallots and thyme sprigs in a roasting tin, then add the olive oil, and coat the shallots evenly using your hands. Roast for about 20–25 minutes or until the shallots are beginning to soften (they should no longer be crunchy).

2 Pour the balsamic vinegar into a stainless steel pan, bring it to a boil, and cook for a few minutes until it reduces. Don't let it cook away for too long, or it will become too sticky. Add the roasted shallots and thyme sprigs, and stir so they all get evenly coated in the reduced vinegar, and the onions are sticky.

3 Spoon the shallots, along with the vinegar and thyme, into a warm sterilized jar with a non-metallic or vinegar-proof lid. Pack the shallots in tightly and top up with extra balsamic vinegar so that the shallots are completely covered. Seal, label, and turn the jar upside down to combine the ingredients thoroughly.

Note Store in a cool, dark place and leave for 2 weeks to mature. Refrigerate after opening. Keeps for 6 months.

SHALLOTS

When to pick
Harvest when the leaves turn yellow, and the shallots are a good size. Leave to dry in the sun for 2 weeks to allow the skins to harden before storing.

Eat and store fresh
Shallots are milder than onions, and can be used where the taste of onions would be too strong. After drying, store in a cool, dark place (see pages 248–9).

How to preserve
Shallots can be used in the same way as onions in pickles, relishes, and chutneys. They can also be chargrilled and preserved whole in oil.

The allium family is indispensible to most cooks, yet we rarely find ways of allowing onions and shallots to take centre stage. This simple lunch recipe gives shallots a starring role.

Caramelized shallot tart

Serves 4–6 • **Prep** 20 mins, plus chilling • **Cooking** 45 mins

INGREDIENTS

25g (scant 1oz) butter

2 tbsp extra virgin olive oil

400g (14oz) shallots, peeled
    and split in half lengthways

2 tbsp balsamic vinegar

a few sprigs of thyme

For the pastry

150g (5¹/₂oz) plain flour

sea salt

75g (2¹/₂oz) butter

or 250g (9oz) ready-made
    shortcrust pastry

METHOD

1 For the pastry, combine the flour, a pinch of salt, and 75g (2¹/₂oz) of the butter in a food processor, and mix to form fine breadcrumbs. With the motor running, add cold water, a tablespoon at a time, until the pastry starts to stick together. Form the pastry into a ball, wrap it in cling film and leave it in the fridge to chill for 30 minutes.

2 Preheat the oven to 200°C (400°F/Gas 6). In a large ovenproof frying pan, melt the remaining butter with the olive oil. Put the shallots in, cut side down, and cook very gently for 10 minutes until they are browned. Turn them over and cook for another 5 minutes. Add the balsamic vinegar and 2 tbsp of water, then remove from the heat. Tuck the thyme sprigs between the shallots.

3 Roll out the pastry to a circle a little larger than the frying pan. Lay the pastry over the shallots, trim, and tuck it in. Transfer the pan to the oven and cook for 30 minutes until the pastry is golden brown.

4 Remove the pan from the oven and bang gently to loosen the shallots. Run a knife around the edges of the pastry, then put a large plate over the pan and quickly turn it over. Serve warm with a green salad.

Curing and storage conditions

Curing Ordinarily, onions, garlic, and shallots must be left to dry out, or "cured", before they can be stored and used for cooking. Once harvested, leave them to cure for 2 weeks in a warm, dry place, or outside in suitable weather on a dry path or on pallets or upturned boxes, turning them to expose all sides to the sun. They are ready to plait and store when the skins are papery and the stems have shrivelled. However, do not let the stems dry so much that they become brittle; there should still be a little moisture at the centre of the stem.

Storing plaits Hang in a well-ventilated, cold room, ideally 1–5°C (33–41°F), to prevent green shoots sprouting from the bulbs. Humidity and lack of ventilation will cause mould.

Storing shallots Harvest and cure shallots in the same way as onions and garlic. Store long-term in nets or boxes somewhere cool and airy, and when needed in the kitchen, move them to a basket or vegetable rack.

3 **Plait the garlic or onions** Set a bulb straight on top, and criss-cross 2 more over that. Divide the stems into 3 strands of 2 stems each and plait. Secure with string.

4 **Hang up to store** Continue to plait the stems, adding 3 new bulbs every time, until you have a plait long enough to hang up. Tie off in a knot at the end.

249

CELERY

When to pick
Pick celery when it is around 30cm (12in) high, after watering. Young celery can be harvested sooner for eating raw, the more mature plants later, for soups and stews.

Eat and store fresh
Eat raw celery as soon as possible, but if necessary, store it in the bottom of the fridge for up to 5 days. Crisp up the stems in cold water before eating.

How to preserve
Celery can be preserved in oil, having been chargrilled first. It is more commonly used as an ingredient in relishes, chutneys, and pickles.

In this salad, the strong tastes of celery and bitter leaves more than hold their own against the pungency of a blue cheese dressing, with the walnuts adding crunch and texture.

Celery and apple salad
with blue cheese dressing

Serves 4 • **Prep** 10 mins • **Cooking** 2 mins

INGREDIENTS

8 tbsp or 60g (2oz) chopped walnuts
300g (10$\frac{1}{2}$oz) blue cheese, such as dolcelatte or gorgonzola
4 tbsp cider vinegar
4 tbsp hazelnut oil or walnut oil
freshly ground black pepper
4 celery sticks, trimmed and sliced diagonally into 1cm ($\frac{1}{2}$in) slices
2 green apples, cored and cut into thin wedges
4 large handfuls of watercress or rocket
sea salt

METHOD

1 In a frying pan or wok, dry fry the walnuts for a couple of minutes until they are golden and crispy. Set aside to cool.

2 In a food processor, mix together 100g (3$\frac{1}{2}$oz) of the blue cheese, vinegar, oil, and a good grinding of black pepper. Whizz it up to a smooth, creamy dressing, which should have thick pouring consistency. Add up to 1 tbsp of cold water to thin the dressing a little, if it is too thick.

3 In a large bowl, mix the celery, apple, and watercress or rocket. Coat the salad with the dressing and check it for seasoning. Top with the walnut pieces and the rest of the blue cheese, crumbled or diced into bite-sized pieces.

This simple yet hearty soup can be prepared with any blue cheese, and the quantities can be easily scaled up or down as required. As with all soups, good quality stock is crucial.

Creamy celery
and Stilton soup

Serves 4 • **Prep** 10 mins • **Cooking** 25 mins

INGREDIENTS

4 celery sticks, chopped

2 potatoes, chopped

1 onion, chopped

hot stock, vegetable or chicken,
    approx. 450ml (15fl oz)

225g (8oz) Stilton cheese,
    crumbled

1 tbsp single cream

sea salt and freshly ground
    black pepper

handful of chives, snipped

METHOD

1 Put the celery, potatoes, and onion in a pan. Pour over the hot stock to cover the vegetables, and simmer gently for 30 minutes until tender.

2 Remove the pan from the heat and leave to cool slightly. Purée the vegetables and stock with the Stilton, using either a hand-held blender or transferring to a food processor. Strain through a sieve to remove any celery strings, return to the pan, and cook gently over low heat. Stir in the single cream.

3 Season to taste and serve immediately, garnished with snipped chives.

An unusual way to cook celery, here the heart is quartered and roasted with orange and walnuts. Delicious served with roast chicken, pork, or a piece of grilled halibut or monkfish.

Roasted celery
with orange and walnuts

Serves 4 • **Prep** 10 mins • **Cooking** 55 mins

INGREDIENTS

4 celery hearts, trimmed
    and quartered
zest and juice of 1 orange
extra virgin olive oil,
    for drizzling
knob of butter, melted
1 tsp caster sugar
sprig of thyme, leaves picked
    and chopped
handful of walnuts, chopped
sea salt and freshly ground
    black pepper

METHOD

1 Preheat the oven to 200°C (400°F/Gas 6). Put the celery hearts in a roasting tin and add the orange zest and juice. Drizzle with a little olive oil and the butter. Sprinkle over the sugar, thyme, and walnuts. Season with salt and pepper to taste.

2 Cover the roasting tin tightly with foil and cook in the oven for 40 minutes. Remove the foil and leave in the oven to brown for a further 15 minutes until tender and glazed. Serve hot or warm.

BEETROOTS

When to pick
Pick beetroots when they are between a golf ball and a tennis ball in size. Larger beetroots keep well in the ground. Some varieties can last until the first frosts, and be harvested as needed.

Eat and store fresh
Eat the tops as soon as possible, either raw in salads or stir-fried. Baby beetroots can be eaten raw, but larger beets need to be cooked. Boil, steam, or roast the roots, and stir-fry the leafy tops.

How to preserve
Use beetroots in pickles, relishes, and chutneys. Beetroots can be stored buried in sand in trays for several months (see page 262).

This deep pink soup is an ideal way to serve large beetroots. Smaller beets can simply be steamed or roasted, but the larger ones often need a little more attention to bring out their flavour.

Beetroot
and apple soup

Serves 6–8 • **Prep** 20 mins • **Cooking** 1 hour

INGREDIENTS

1 onion, halved

2 garlic cloves

3 tbsp extra virgin olive oil

salt and freshly ground
    black pepper

350g (12oz) raw beetroot,
    peeled and halved

1 potato, halved

4 dessert apples, peeled
    and cored

1.5 litres (2¾ pints) hot
    vegetable stock or
    chicken stock

1–2 tbsp soft dark brown sugar

juice of 1 lemon

2 tbsp finely chopped parsley,
    chives, dill, or coriander,
    or a mixture

200g (7oz) crème fraîche or
    plain yogurt

METHOD

1 Grate the onion and garlic in a food processor. Heat the oil in a large pan over low heat, add the onion, garlic, and a pinch of salt. Cook gently, stirring once or twice, for 5 minutes or until soft. Meanwhile, grate the beetroot, potato, and apples, in the food processor.

2 Add the beetroot, potato, and apples to the pan and stew gently for 10 minutes, stirring occasionally. Pour in the stock, bring to a boil, then cover with a lid and simmer gently for 45 minutes or until the beetroot is cooked through.

3 Blend with a hand-held blender or transfer to a food processor and whizz. You may need to do this in batches. Season with the sugar, lemon juice, and some salt and pepper.

4 Stir the chopped herbs into the crème fraîche or yogurt, then ladle the soup into warm bowls and drop a big spoonful of the crème fraîche or yogurt into the middle of the soup.

This brightly coloured risotto is amazing when cooked with freshly harvested beetroots. The deep, earthy flavour of the beetroot and the sharp tang of goat's cheese combine beautifully.

Beetroot risotto

Serves 4 • **Prep** 30 mins • **Cooking** 1 hour

INGREDIENTS

500g (1lb 2oz) beetroot, peeled and diced

2 tbsp extra virgin olive oil, plus extra for tossing

sea salt and freshly ground black pepper

6 tbsp sunflower oil

20 sage leaves

2 medium onions, finely diced

2 garlic cloves, crushed

350g (12oz) risotto rice

1 litre (1³/₄ pints) vegetable or chicken stock

60g (2oz) Parmesan cheese, grated

200g (7oz) firm goat's cheese, cut into 1cm (¹/₂in) dice

METHOD

1 Preheat the oven to 200°C (400°F/Gas 6). Toss the beetroot in a little olive oil, salt, and pepper. Wrap in foil and cook in the oven for 30–40 minutes until soft.

2 In a small pan, heat the sunflower oil over high heat until smoking. Drop in most of the sage leaves, a few at a time, and deep fry for 5 seconds, or until they stop fizzing, remove, and drain.

3 Remove the beetroot from the oven and purée in a food processor with 4 tablespoons of water, the remaining sage leaves, and some salt and pepper. Set aside.

4 Fry the onions in the olive oil over moderate heat for 3 minutes, until soft. Add the garlic and cook for 1 minute. Pour in the rice and stir so that the grains are coated in oil.

5 Keeping the stock on a low simmer, add a ladle at a time to the rice, stirring continuously until each ladleful is absorbed, for about 15 minutes until the rice is almost cooked. Add the beetroot purée to the risotto and cook for another 5–10 minutes until the rice is soft.

6 Remove the rice from the heat, season, then stir in two-thirds of the Parmesan and fold in the goat's cheese. Serve garnished with the sage leaves and Parmesan.

The sweet, earthy flavours of the beetroots and sweet potatoes used here work beautifully with the peppery beef. Cook your beetroots in boiling water until tender then peel before roasting.

Peppered beef
with balsamic-roasted beetroot

Serves 4 • **Prep** 15 mins • **Cooking** 1 hour–1 hour 50 mins

INGREDIENTS

4 medium beetroots

1.1kg (2½lb) fillet of beef

1–2 tbsp cracked black pepper

2–3 tbsp extra virgin olive oil

1 tbsp good-quality
    balsamic vinegar

4 sweet potatoes, peeled
    and quartered

salt

handful of thyme sprigs

creamed horseradish, to taste

METHOD

1 Place the beetroots in a saucepan, cover with water, and bring to a boil. Simmer for 45 minutes to 1 hour or until tender. Drain, leave to cool, peel, and chop into quarters.

2 Preheat the oven to 190°C (375°F/Gas 5). Roll the beef in the pepper, covering it all over. Put 1 tablespoon of the oil in a roasting tin and set the tin over high heat. When very hot, add the beef, and cook for 5–6 minutes, or until lightly browned on all sides.

3 Toss the beetroots with the balsamic vinegar and add to the tin. Toss the sweet potatoes with the remaining oil and add to the tin. Season with a pinch of salt, sprinkle with the thyme, and put in the oven to cook for about 20 minutes for rare beef, 40 minutes for medium, and 50 minutes for well done.

4 Remove the beef from the oven and keep it warm. Continue cooking the vegetables until they are golden and slightly charred. Slice the beef and serve with the beetroots, sweet potatoes, and creamed horseradish.

This sweet relish with a hint of spice is perfect to serve with cheese or cold cuts. If you want to save time making the relish, you can cook the beetroots the night before.

Beetroot relish

Makes 1kg (2¼lb) or 3 medium jars • **Cooking** 2 hours 15 mins

INGREDIENTS

1.35kg (3lb) beetroots

1 tsp caster sugar

450g (1lb) shallots,
    finely chopped

600ml (1 pint) cider vinegar,
    or white wine vinegar

1 tbsp pickling spices, placed
    in a muslin spice bag

450g (1lb) caster or granulated
    sugar

METHOD

1 Put the beetroots in a preserving pan or a large heavy, stainless steel saucepan. Pour over enough water to cover them, and add the caster sugar. Bring to a boil and simmer for 1 hour or until the beetroots are soft and cooked. Drain and leave to cool. When cool enough to handle, peel and dice into small, neat pieces.

2 Put the shallots and vinegar in the rinsed preserving pan or saucepan and cook for 10 minutes on low heat. Add the chopped beetroots and the muslin bag of pickling spices. Give the mixture a stir, add the sugar, and cook gently until the sugar has dissolved. Bring to a boil and cook at a rolling boil for 5 minutes, then reduce the heat to a simmer and cook for about 40 minutes or until the mixture thickens.

3 Remove the spice bag, then ladle into warm, sterilized jars with non-metallic or vinegar-proof lids, making sure there are no air gaps. Seal, label, and store in a cool, dark place. Allow the flavours to mature for 1 month, and refrigerate after opening.

Note Keeps for 9 months unopened.

Store crops naturally

Storing crops in their natural state in a cool, protected environment, is the next best thing to picking produce fresh from the allotment. It allows you to extend an autumn harvest from the allotment or garden. Low-tech methods such as storing in trays or boxes, hanging produce, and storing on shelves in cool rooms, mean that treasured home-grown fruit and vegetables can be savoured and enjoyed for months to come.

Storing beetroots in trays

1 **Cleaning and trimming** Cut off leaves and remove soil with a brush. Don't brush too hard, however, or trim the roots as cuts could cause rot.

2 **Burying in sand** Fill the bottom of a tray with sand, layer the beetroots on top so they are not touching, and cover with more sand. Store in a cool room or root cellar.

Other options for natural storage

Some crops can be stored in clamps or in the ground (see pages 140–1); other options include hanging indoors or storing in boxes.

In boxes Crops including carrots, parsnips, potatoes, swedes, turnips, celeriac, and kohl rabi buried in compost or sand, in boxes, in a cool, ambient store room (see pages 268–9).

Hanging indoors Dried or "cured" pumpkins, squashes, garlic, onions, and shallots can be hung in nets, allowing the air to circulate around them.

Tips on storing crops

To keep your produce in tip-top condition it is vital to select suitable crops, store them properly, and monitor any deterioration.

Select best produce Only store the best quality crops. Damaged crops spread disease.
Handle carefully Bruising of crops leads to rot.
Storage conditions Avoid damp spaces and extremes of temperatures.
Check regularly Remove any crops showing signs of disease immediately.

Storing pumpkins

1 **"Curing" the fruit** Cut off the squash leaving 10–15cm (4–6in) of stem. Leave outside so that the skin hardens. "Cure" in the sun for 7–10 days, turning regularly.

2 **Store in a cool room** Put on a raised shelf or hang in a net bag where air can circulate. They will keep for months but check regularly for signs of deterioration.

CARROTS

When to pick
Harvest from 10 weeks after planting to eat raw. Carrots for cooking can be left in the ground for longer and harvested as needed until winter sets in.

Eat and store fresh
Eat young carrots washed but unpeeled, in salads. Store larger carrots in the fridge, or in boxes for 2 months or more (see pages 268–9).

How to preserve
Use carrots as an ingredient in chutneys, pickles, and relishes.

Freezing options
Wash, peel, chop, and blanch for 2–3 minutes, then cool and freeze for up to 6 months.

This richly-coloured salad is more than just pretty; it's packed with beneficial antioxidants too. Choose young, fresh vegetables as they are best eaten raw straight from the allotment.

Carrot and beetroot salad
with balsamic vinaigrette

Serves 4–6 • Prep 30 mins • Cooking 3–4 mins

INGREDIENTS

600g (1lb 5oz) carrots, trimmed and scrubbed
1 bunch beetroots, approx. 600g (1lb 5oz), peeled and halved
small bunch of parsley, chopped, or salad cress, snipped

For the vinaigrette
6 tbsp extra virgin olive oil, plus 1 tsp for toasting the seeds
50ml (2fl oz) balsamic vinegar
1 garlic clove, crushed (optional)
50g (1³/₄oz) sunflower or pumpkin seeds
1 tsp soy sauce (optional)
salt and freshly ground black pepper

METHOD

1 Coarsely grate the raw vegetables and combine in a large bowl.

2 For the vinaigrette, put the oil, vinegar, and garlic (if using), in a screw-top jar, put the lid on tightly and shake.

3 Gently heat the remaining teaspoon of olive oil in a small frying pan and toast the seeds for 3–4 minutes over moderate heat, stirring frequently to prevent sticking. Add the soy sauce at the end of cooking (if using). Most of the soy sauce will evaporate, leaving a salty taste and extra browning for the seeds.

4 Add the parsley or cress to the carrot and beetroot. Shake the vinaigrette again, pour over the vegetables, then season to taste. Toss the salad gently, scatter the toasted seeds over and serve.

Note The vegetables, vinaigrette, and seeds can be prepared and stored separately in the fridge for up to 24 hours. Return to room temperature and combine before serving.

A light, refreshing soup with a hint of spice, this is the perfect start to a summer meal. Use fresh, young carrots and try adding a swirl of cream or plain yogurt before serving.

Spicy carrot
and orange soup

Serves 4 • **Prep** 10 mins • **Cooking** 45 mins

INGREDIENTS

2 tsp light olive oil or
   sunflower oil
1 leek, sliced
500g (1lb 2oz) carrots,
   trimmed, scrubbed,
   and sliced
1 potato, about 115g (4oz),
   chopped
1/2 tsp ground coriander
pinch of ground cumin
300ml (10fl oz) orange juice
500ml (16fl oz) vegetable
   or chicken stock
1 bay leaf
sea salt and freshly ground
   black pepper
2 tbsp chopped coriander,
   to garnish

METHOD

1 Place the oil, leek, and carrots in a large saucepan and cook over low heat for 5 minutes, stirring frequently, or until the leek has softened. Add the potato, coriander, and cumin, then pour in the orange juice and stock and stir. Add the bay leaf and season with salt and pepper.

2 Increase the heat, bring the soup to a boil, then lower the heat, cover, and simmer for 40 minutes, or until the vegetables are very tender.

3 Allow the soup to cool slightly, then purée to a smooth consistency using a hand-held blender or by transferring to a food processor, working in batches if necessary.

4 Return to the saucepan and add a little extra stock or water if the soup is too thick. Bring back to a simmer, then transfer to heated serving bowls and sprinkle with chopped coriander.

Note The soup can be stored in the freezer for up to 3 months.

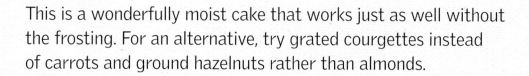

This is a wonderfully moist cake that works just as well without the frosting. For an alternative, try grated courgettes instead of carrots and ground hazelnuts rather than almonds.

Carrot cake
with soft cheese frosting

Serves 12–14 • **Prep** 30 mins • **Cooking** 35–40 mins

INGREDIENTS

For the cake

1 large orange

225g (8oz) butter, softened

225g (8oz) light soft
brown sugar

4 large eggs

115g (4oz) wholemeal flour

85g (3oz) self-raising flour

2 tsp baking powder

1 tsp ground mixed spice

60g (2oz) ground almonds

2 large carrots, trimmed,
scrubbed, and grated,
about 300g (10^1/$_2$oz)

For the frosting

225g (8oz) cream cheese

grated zest and juice
of ^{1}/$_2$ orange

75g (2^1/$_2$oz) icing sugar, sifted

METHOD

1 Preheat the oven to 180°C (350°F/Gas 4). Grease two 20cm (8in) sandwich tins and line with baking parchment. Thinly pare the zest of half the orange, cut into thin strips and boil in water for 2 minutes. Drain and set aside. Finely grate the remaining zest and squeeze the juice.

2 Cream the butter and sugar together until light and fluffy. Add the eggs, and the zest and juice of the orange, and whisk thoroughly. Add the remaining cake ingredients, except the carrots, and beat well with a wooden spoon. Fold in the carrots.

3 Spoon the mixture into the tins. Bake in the oven for 35–40 minutes until golden and firm to the touch. Turn out onto a wire rack, remove the paper, and leave to cool.

4 To make the frosting, mix the cheese with the orange zest and icing sugar. Work in just enough orange juice until the frosting mix forms soft peaks. Sandwich the cake together with half the frosting and spread the remainder over the top. Decorate with the reserved strips of orange zest.

Store root crops in boxes

Many root vegetables can be left in situ through the winter months, but it may be more convenient to lift and store them inside. They will also be less prone to damage caused by frost, disease, and pests. Carrots, parsnips, beetroots, and potatoes, among others, can be stored in boxes. Only store the best produce to prevent disease spreading. Keep in a cool, dark place such as a garage or spare room for two months or more. Use as required and keep remaining vegetables covered.

1 **Preparing the carrots** Harvest on a dry day, shake off excess soil, and twist off the tops. Don't scrub or wash the carrots, as this may damage the skin.

2 **Line the box** Line a shallow box with newspaper or sacking. Cover with a thin layer of spent compost, moist sand, coir, untreated sawdust, vermiculite, or leaf mould.

Store Carrots

YOU WILL NEED

carrots

shallow box

newspaper or sacking

spent compost, sand, coir,
  untreated sawdust,
  vermiculite or leaf mould

Storing potatoes in boxes

If you haven't got a large garden or don't own an allotment that can accommodate potato clamps (see pages 140–1), store crops of potatoes in tea chests or cardboard boxes with covers on top to block the light. These covers are essential, or the potatoes will turn green (the green parts are toxic, and must be cut away). Alternatively, store them in strong paper sacks, folded or tied loosely at the top. Store the potatoes in a cool, dark place (5–10°C/41–50°F). Cut away any sprouts before eating.

3 **Position the first layer** Arrange the carrots side by side on the compost so that they are not touching. Position the carrots so that they lie head to toe.

4 **Cover and repeat** Add another layer of compost over the carrots and repeat until the container is full. Finish with a layer of compost to block light and close the box.

When to pick
Sweet potatoes grow well in warm climates and take around 4–5 months to mature. Harvest them when the foliage starts to wilt and turn yellow.

Eat and store fresh
They can be stored in the fridge for up to 1 week or stored like ordinary potatoes (see pages 140–1). Delicious baked, roasted, or thinly sliced and chargrilled to accompany chicken or fish dishes.

Freezing options
Griddle slices and open freeze on trays, or freeze as a cooked purée, for up to 9 months.

The inspiration for this dish comes from a classic Japanese dish known as *daigakuimo*. It is a wonderfully simple recipe that turns the humble sweet potato into something special.

Soy and sesame glazed
sweet potatoes

Serves 4 • **Prep** 10 mins • **Cooking** 40 mins

INGREDIENTS

2 tbsp soy sauce

2 tbsp light soft brown sugar

2 tbsp rice wine

1 tbsp sesame oil

2 garlic cloves, crushed

500g (1lb 2oz) sweet potatoes, peeled and cut into wedges

1 tbsp toasted sesame seeds

METHOD

1 Preheat the oven to 200°C (400°F/Gas 6). Put all the ingredients except the sweet potatoes and sesame seeds in a small saucepan. Bring to a boil, reduce the heat and simmer for 2 minutes.

2 Put the potato wedges on a baking tray or ovenproof serving dish and pour the sauce mixture over them, tossing well. Scatter the sesame seeds over the top and cover the baking tray or dish with foil.

3 Cook for 20 minutes then turn the oven up to 220°C (425°F/Gas 7). Remove the foil and cook for another 20 minutes. Turn the potatoes several times while cooking until they have absorbed all the sauce and are soft, glazed, and sticky. These are superb eaten alongside a piece of grilled mackerel with some wilted greens.

The vegetables for this soup are cooked in the oven, which brings out their naturally sweet flavours. The harissa adds depth and a spicy edge. Delicious served with warm pitta bread.

Moroccan roasted
sweet potato soup

Serves 4 • **Prep** 20 mins • **Cooking** 50 mins

INGREDIENTS

675g (1½lb) sweet potatoes, peeled and cut into big chunks

6 large shallots, quartered

3 plump garlic cloves, unpeeled

1 carrot, cut into big chunks

1 tbsp harissa, plus extra to serve

2 tbsp extra virgin olive oil

salt and freshly ground black pepper

900ml (1½ pints) hot vegetable stock

1 tsp clear honey

generous squeeze of lemon juice

natural yogurt, to serve

pitta bread, to serve

METHOD

1 Preheat the oven to 200°C (400°F/Gas 6). Put the sweet potatoes, shallots, garlic, and carrot in a roasting tin. Mix the harissa with the oil, then pour over the vegetables and toss together so they are coated well. Season with black pepper, then roast, turning occasionally, for 40 minutes or until tender and turning golden. Remove from the oven.

2 Squeeze the garlic cloves out of their skins into the roasting tin. Stir in the stock and honey, then scrape up all the bits from the bottom of the tin. Carefully transfer to a blender and whizz until smooth. You may need to do this in batches. Pour into a saucepan and reheat gently.

3 Add the lemon juice and season to taste with salt and pepper. Swirl the yogurt with a little harissa and top each bowl with a spoonful. Serve with warm pitta bread.

A simple one-pot dish, the sweet-spicy sauce works wonderfully well with the earthiness of the sweet potatoes. Sweet potatoes can break up easily, so be sure that they don't cook for too long.

Garlic and chilli chicken
with honeyed sweet potatoes

Serves 4 • **Prep** 15 mins • **Cooking** 1 ¼ hours

INGREDIENTS

8 chicken pieces (a mixture
    of thighs and drumsticks),
    skin on
salt and freshly ground
    black pepper
4 sweet potatoes, peeled and
    cut into big chunks
1–2 tbsp clear honey
2 tbsp extra virgin olive oil
2 medium-hot red chillies,
    deseeded and sliced
a few sprigs of thyme
½ garlic bulb, cloves separated,
    peeled, and smashed
1 small glass of dry white wine
300ml (10fl oz) light
    chicken stock

METHOD

1 Preheat the oven to 200°C (400°F/Gas 6). Season the chicken liberally with salt and black pepper, and coat the sweet potatoes in the honey.

2 In a heavy flameproof casserole, preferably cast-iron, heat 1 tablespoon of the oil over medium heat. Add the sweet potatoes and cook, stirring, for about 5 minutes until beginning to colour; the honey should caramelize but not burn. Remove from the casserole and set aside.

3 Increase the heat to medium-high, and heat the remaining oil in the same casserole. Brown the chicken for about 5 minutes on each side until nicely golden all over. Add the chillies, thyme, and garlic. Return the sweet potatoes to the casserole, and season well.

4 Pour in the wine and stock, cover the casserole, and transfer to the oven to cook for 1 hour. Check the casserole a few times during cooking; give it a stir if needed, or add a small amount of stock if it is too dry. Serve hot with chunks of fresh crusty bread.

This delicious autumnal dish makes a great accompaniment to a traditional roast, but is equally good scattered over some bitter leaves and eaten as a warm winter salad.

Squash with cranberries
and chestnuts

Serves 4 • **Prep** 10 mins • **Cooking** 30 mins

INGREDIENTS

1–2 tbsp extra virgin olive oil

knob of butter

pinch of allspice

pinch of cinnamon

1 butternut squash, peeled, halved, deseeded, and cut into bite-sized pieces

salt and freshly ground black pepper

200g packet ready-cooked chestnuts

50g (1³/₄oz) cranberries

sugar, to taste (optional)

METHOD

1 Preheat the oven to 200°C (400°F/Gas 6). Heat the oil and butter in a large frying pan, add the allspice, cinnamon, and squash. Season well with salt and pepper, and cook over low-medium heat, stirring occasionally, for 15 minutes, or until the squash begins to soften a little. Add a little more oil, if needed.

2 Add the chestnuts and stir so they are coated with the oil. Cook over low heat for 5–10 minutes, then add the cranberries and cook for 5 minutes more.

3 Taste, and season again, if needed, adding a little sugar if the cranberries are too tart (cook until the sugar has dissolved).

CRANBERRIES

When to pick
Pick cranberries at the end of summer, when the fruits are dark red, glossy, and bursting with juice. Leave on the bush and harvest as needed.

Eat and store fresh
Cranberries can be eaten raw, but they are extremely tart. They can be stored in the fridge for 3–5 days and cooked in pies or compôtes.

How to preserve
Cranberries are traditionally preserved in cranberry sauce (see page 276). They can also be used in jams and jellies, savoury chutneys, and relishes.

Freezing options
Open freeze whole on trays, as a cooked or uncooked purée, or blanched or poached in sugar syrup (see pages 194–5).

A classic accompaniment to roast turkey at Christmas time, making your own cranberry sauce is a simple affair and tastes far superior to anything you would buy.

Cranberry sauce

Makes 300ml (10fl oz) • **Prep** 5 mins • **Cooking** 15 mins

INGREDIENTS

250g (9oz) cranberries
1 small shallot, finely chopped
100g (3¹/₂oz) light
   muscovado sugar
zest and juice of 1 orange
4 tbsp red wine or port

METHOD

1 Put the cranberries in a saucepan with the shallot, sugar, orange zest and juice, and red wine. Bring to a boil, stirring, until the sugar has dissolved.

2 Simmer gently for 10–12 minutes, or until the cranberries are beginning to break up.

3 Leave to cool, then transfer to a serving dish or storage jar.

Note Cranberry sauce is good served with turkey, or other poultry. This sweet sauce can also be served with ice cream. Keep refrigerated for up to 1 week and frozen for up to 2 months.

The fresh grapes and sweet white wine used here complement the rich flavour of the partridge breasts. Keep the partridge legs and use in a slow-cooked stew for another day.

Roast partridge breasts
with grapes in Sauternes

Serves 6 • **Prep** 30 mins, plus soaking • **Cooking** 35 mins

INGREDIENTS

6 whole partridges

60g (2oz) butter

12 sage leaves

12 rashers of rindless
    streaky bacon, or slices
    of Parma ham

extra virgin olive oil,
    for browning

For the sauce

2 shallots, finely chopped

360ml (12fl oz) Sauternes, or
    other sweet white wine

360ml (12fl oz) chicken stock

115g (4oz) white seedless
    grapes, sliced in half

30g (1oz) butter, chilled
    and diced

METHOD

1 Pour the Sauternes over the grape halves and leave to soak for at least 1 hour.

2 Cut the breasts off the partridges. Place a knob of butter and sage leaf on the underside of each partridge breast, then wrap with 1 slice of bacon.

3 Melt a little olive oil in a frying pan over high heat and brown the wrapped partridge breasts on both sides. Place them in a roasting tin and set aside.

4 Preheat the oven to 190°C (375°F/Gas 5). To make the sauce, fry the shallots in the same frying pan until soft, adding more oil if needed. Strain the Sauternes into the pan, reserving the grapes. Bring to a boil, simmer for 10 minutes, or until the wine is reduced, then add the stock, and bring back to a boil. Reduce the sauce again, add the grapes, and simmer gently until ready to serve.

5 Roast the partridge breasts for 12 minutes, turning once. Bring the sauce back to a gentle simmer, and whisk in the butter. Serve the partridge with the sauce.

GRAPES

When to pick
Leave grapes on the vine as long as possible, until they are sweet and juicy, but before the skin shrivels. The longer they are left to mature, the sweeter they will be.

Eat and store fresh
Keep grapes at room temperature and eat raw within 3–5 days of picking.

How to preserve
Apart from being the main ingredient in wine, grapes can also be used in jams, jellies, and pickles, as well as being made into cordials and syrups.

This delightful cake can either be served warm as a dessert with cream or custard, or eaten cold with a cup of coffee. The grapes turn into a layer of sticky fruit on top of the cake and keep it moist.

Red grape
and cinnamon cake

Serves 6–8 • **Prep** 30 mins • **Cooking** 50 mins

INGREDIENTS

300g (10^1/$_2$oz) red grapes, halved lengthways
2 tbsp light soft brown sugar
150g (5^1/$_2$oz) caster sugar
150g (5^1/$_2$oz) butter, softened
3 eggs
^{1}/$_2$ tsp natural vanilla extract
150g (5^1/$_2$oz) self-raising flour
1 tsp cinnamon
1 heaped tsp baking powder

METHOD

1 Preheat the oven to 180°C (350°F/Gas 4). Line a 20cm (8in) loose-bottomed cake tin with greaseproof paper. Spread the grapes evenly, skin side down, on the bottom of the cake tin and scatter over the brown sugar.

2 In a blender or food processor, cream together the caster sugar and butter. When the mixture is smooth, add the eggs and vanilla extract, and mix well. Add the flour, cinnamon, and baking powder, and pulse the mixture briefly until it is blended.

3 Spread the sponge mixture over the grapes. Place the cake tin on a baking tray and bake in the centre of the oven for approximately 50 minutes, until risen and golden brown, and a skewer through the middle comes out clean. Turn the cake out onto a serving plate, carefully peeling the greaseproof paper to reveal the grape topping. Serve warm with some vanilla custard, thick cream, or yogurt.

Note The cake will keep for 2–3 days in an airtight container.

Make jelly

The queen of preserves, jelly is made from the strained juice of fruit which produces clear, jewel-like results. Use perfect fruit, slightly under-ripe, and boil for the minimum time to achieve a set. Prolonged boiling is detrimental and may mean the jelly will not set. The quantity of strained juice always varies so calculate the sugar after measuring the juice. Allow 450g (1lb) of sugar for every 600ml (1 pint) of juice. Adding the lemon ensures there is enough pectin to achieve a set. Store in a cool, dark place and keep refrigerated once opened.

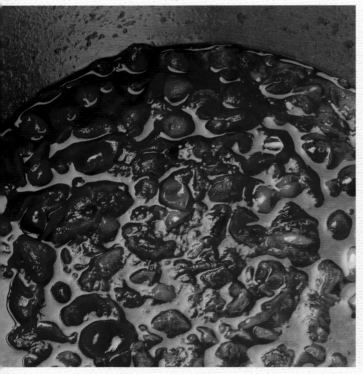

1 **Cook the grapes** Put the fruit and lemon in a preserving pan or large heavy saucepan with the water. Bring to a boil, cover, and cook gently for 35–40 minutes.

2 **Remove the pulp** Strain the fruit through a jelly bag or clean nylon sieve over a clean bowl. Measure the juice and calculate the quantity of sugar (see above).

If you have an apple tree you probably have everything else you need for this simple yet delicious dessert in your kitchen cupboard, making it an ideal standby recipe.

Apple brown betty

Serves 4 • **Prep** 30 mins • **Cooking** 35–45 mins

INGREDIENTS

85g (3oz) butter

175g (6oz) fresh breadcrumbs

900g (2lb) apples, such as
  Bramley, Granny Smith,
  or Golden Delicious

85g (3oz) soft light brown
  sugar

1 tsp ground cinnamon

$^1/_2$ tsp mixed spice

zest of 1 lemon

2 tbsp lemon juice

1 tsp natural vanilla extract

METHOD

1 Preheat the oven to 180°C (350°F/Gas 4). Melt the butter in a saucepan, add the breadcrumbs, and mix well.

2 Peel, quarter, and core the apples. Cut into slices and place in a bowl. Add the sugar, cinnamon, mixed spice, lemon zest and juice, and vanilla extract, and mix well.

3 Put half the apple mixture into a 1.2 litre (2 pint) baking dish. Cover with half the breadcrumbs, then put in the rest of the apples and top with the rest of the breadcrumbs.

4 Bake for 35–45 minutes, checking after 35 minutes. If it is getting too brown, reduce the oven temperature to 160°C (325°F/Gas 3), and cover with greaseproof paper. It is cooked when the crumbs are golden brown and the apples are soft. Serve warm.

This substantial, adaptable chutney gets better with age and should be left for at least a month before opening. For a darker result use light or dark brown sugar instead of white sugar.

Apple chutney
with dates and raisins

Makes 1.8kg (4lb) or 5 medium jars • **Prep** 45 mins • **Cooking** 1 1/2 hours

INGREDIENTS

2kg (4^1/$_2$lb) cooking apples
   (approx. 8–10), peeled,
   cored, and chopped
3 onions, peeled, and
   finely chopped
2.5cm (1in) piece of root
   ginger, peeled, and
   finely chopped
115g (4oz) sultanas
125g (4^1/$_2$oz) ready-to-eat
   stoned dates, chopped
1 tsp mustard seeds
1 litre (1^3/$_4$ pints) cider vinegar
500g (1lb 2oz) caster or
   granulated sugar

METHOD

1 Put the apples, onions, ginger, sultanas, dates, and mustard seeds in a preserving pan or a large heavy, stainless steel saucepan. Stir everything together, then pour in the cider vinegar and add the sugar.

2 Cook on low heat, stirring until the sugar has dissolved, then bring to a boil, reduce the heat, and cook gently for about 1^1/$_2$ hours. Stir continuously near the end of cooking time so that the chutney doesn't catch on the base of the pan. The mixture is ready when it is thick and sticky.

3 Ladle into warm, sterilized jars with non-metallic or vinegar-proof lids, making sure there are no air gaps. Cover each jar with a waxed paper disc, seal, and label.

Note Store in a cool, dark place. Allow the flavours to mature for 1 month, and refrigerate after opening. Keeps for 9 months unopened.

Oven-dry fruits

Dried fruits make healthy snacks and are an excellent addition to mueslis, baked goods, sauces, pies, and many savoury and sweet dishes. Choose ripe fruits, as they dry quickly and have a better flavour. The same recipe works for many other fruits including tropical fruits, cherries, cranberries, grapes, nectarines, and plums. Keep the oven on its lowest setting and dry for 8–24 hours, depending on the temperature and preferred texture; leave longer for a crunchier version.

1 **Core the apples** Briefly wash the apples in cold water, then core and slice them into 3–5mm (⅛–¼in) rings. Discard the top and bottom rings with the most skin on.

2 **Prevent browning** In a bowl, add the lemon juice or citric acid to 600ml (1 pint) water. Drop in the apples, drain on a tea towel, and place on wire racks over baking trays.

Recipe Dried apples

Makes approx. 115–225g (4–8oz) • **Prep** 15–20 mins, plus drying and cooling • **Keeps** 6 months, if dried properly (12 months frozen)

INGREDIENTS

1kg (2¼lb) ripe dessert
   apples, with bruised or
   damaged areas removed
2 tbsp lemon juice or
   ½ tsp citric acid

Drying different fruits

Keep the door of an electric oven ajar with a skewer to create airflow so that the fruit is dried rather than cooked.

Stoned fruit Remove the stones first.
Fruits with rind Remove thick rind and peel.
Fruits with whole skins Dip fruits with skins left on, such as grapes and cherries, into boiling water for 30 seconds to split the skins first.
Larger fruits Cut fruits like peaches and large figs in half, and dry them cut-side up.

3 **Dry in the oven** Dry for 8–24 hours in the oven at 50–60°C (120–140°F/Gas ¼), turning occasionally, until they look and feel like soft chamois leather.

4 **Store in jars** Remove from the oven, cover with kitchen paper and leave for 24 hours, turning occasionally. Pack into airtight, sterilized jars and store in a cool, dark place.

PEARS

When to pick
Harvest pears when they come away from the tree easily. Cooking pears should be picked when slightly under-ripe, dessert pears can be left a little longer.

Eat and store fresh
Eat dessert pears when slightly soft. Store cooking pears wrapped in paper or in a single layer (without touching) in a cool, dark place for 2–3 months. Check them regularly.

How to preserve
Pears can be used in jams and jellies, chutneys, and pickles.

Freezing options
Freeze for up to 9 months as a cooked purée, or poached and covered with syrup in freezer pots (see pages 194–5).

Pears are delicious served in sweet desserts, but they also work well with strong, savoury flavours. Salty Parma ham and bitter crunchy chicory make a perfect foil for the soft, ripe fruit.

Parma ham
with pears and nectarines

Serves 4 • **Prep** 15 mins

INGREDIENTS

2–3 heads chicory, leaves
    separated and rinsed
3 sweet, ripe pears,
    cored and sliced
3 sweet, ripe nectarines,
    halved, destoned, and sliced
12 slices Parma ham
handful of almonds (skins on)

For the dressing

90ml (3fl oz) extra virgin
    olive oil
2 tbsp apple juice
1 tbsp balsamic vinegar
salt and freshly ground
    black pepper

METHOD

1 First, make the dressing. Put the oil, apple juice, and balsamic vinegar in a jug or small bowl, and whisk together. Season well with salt and black pepper.

2 Arrange the chicory leaves in a single layer on a large serving platter, and drizzle over a little of the dressing.

3 Arrange the fruit slices over the chicory leaves with the Parma ham, and toss together gently. Scatter over the almonds, then drizzle with a little more dressing. Season again, to taste. Serve immediately with some fresh crusty bread.

You can easily produce this tasty cake from some ripe pears and a few storecupboard ingredients. The fruit will keep the cake moist for several days.

Pear and ginger
upside down cake

Serves 6 • **Prep** 5 mins • **Cooking** 20 mins

INGREDIENTS

115g (4oz) butter at room
temperature, plus extra
for greasing

115g (4oz) light brown sugar,
plus extra for sprinkling

2 pears, peeled, cored,
and halved

2 eggs, lightly beaten

115g (4oz) wholemeal
self-raising flour

2 tsp ground ginger

1 tsp baking powder

METHOD

1 Preheat the oven to 190°C (375°F/Gas 5). Thickly grease a 20cm (8in) sandwich tin with butter and sprinkle a little sugar liberally over the top.

2 Lay the pear halves attractively in the tin on top of the sugar.

3 In a bowl, whisk together the butter and sugar until light and creamy. Whisk in the eggs a little at a time, then fold in the flour, ginger, and baking powder with a metal spoon. Spread the mixture over the pears and bake for 20 minutes until just firm. Leave to cool in the tin for 5 minutes, then transfer to a wire rack to cool. Serve warm with cream or custard.

This impressive dinner party dessert is made with a few simple ingredients. Prepare a day in advance to allow the colours and flavours of the sauce to soak into the fruit. Serve with ice cream.

Pears poached
in red wine and thyme

Serves 4 • **Prep** 20–30 mins • **Cooking** 50 mins, plus cooling

INGREDIENTS

750ml (1¼ pints) red wine

200g (7oz) caster sugar

2 sprigs of thyme

1 cinnamon stick

1 orange

4 firm dessert pears

METHOD

1 Mix the wine, sugar, thyme, and cinnamon stick in a pan just big enough to hold the 4 pears. Bring to the boil and reduce to a simmer.

2 Using a peeler, remove the zest of the orange in large slivers and add to the pan. Cut the orange in half and squeeze the juice into the pan.

3 Peel the pears, leaving the stalks intact, but slicing off the base of each pear to leave a flat surface for standing. Add the pears to the pan, topping up with water, if necessary, to cover them. Simmer over low heat, covered, for 20 minutes or until the fruit is soft. Leave to cool in the liquid and refrigerate overnight.

4 Before serving, remove the pears from the liquid and return to the heat. Bring to a boil and simmer to reduce to a depth of 1cm (½in), or until thickened and slightly sticky. Taste the sauce, to make sure the flavours are strong, but not burnt. Strain and serve the cold pears with the hot sauce poured over.

When to pick
Pick quinces when golden yellow in colour, and when they come away easily from the branch. They are a very hard fruit, so do not wait for them to soften.

Eat and store fresh
Quinces can be kept for several weeks in a cool, dark place before cooking.

How to preserve
The traditional Spanish preserve, membrillo (see right), is a well-known way of preserving quinces, but they can also be used in jams, jellies, and pickles.

Freezing options
Best frozen as a cooked purée, or blanched or poached in sugar syrup (see pages 194–5).

This Spanish preserve is a fruit cheese made with quinces. Quince trees are often old and productive, but the fruits cannot be eaten raw. This is one of the best ways to unlock their subtle flavour.

Membrillo

Makes approx. 750g–1kg (1lb 10oz–2¼lb) • **Prep** 10 mins • **Cooking** 1½ hours

INGREDIENTS

1kg (2¼lb) quinces, scrubbed
    and roughly chopped
juice of ½ lemon
approx. 450g (1lb) caster
    or granulated sugar
    (see method)
oil, for greasing

METHOD

1 Place the quinces in a preserving pan or a large, heavy stainless steel saucepan with 600ml (1 pint) of water. Add the lemon juice, bring to a boil, and simmer for 30 minutes. When soft, crush the fruit into a pulp with a potato masher. Leave to one side to cool.

2 Sieve the pulp in batches over a large, clean bowl, pressing hard against the sieve with a wooden spoon. Measure the purée: for every 450ml (15fl oz), add 450g (1lb) of sugar. Put the purée and sugar back in the pan and stir over low heat to dissolve the sugar.

3 Bring to a boil. Simmer gently for 45–60 minutes or longer. The purée will reduce down to a dark, thick, glossy paste. It is ready when it makes a "plopping" noise and sticks to the wooden spoon.

4 Grease 6 warm sterilized ramekin dishes or moulds with a little oil. Spoon in the paste and level the top. Seal with waxed paper discs and cellophane if leaving in the ramekin dishes, otherwise leave to cool. Loosen with a palette knife, turn out, and wrap in waxed paper.

Note Leave to mature in a cool, dark place for 4–6 weeks. Keeps for 12 months.

The quince is a relative of the pear and apple, with a similar shape, but a bitter taste until cooked. Try these bottled quinces as a dessert with cream or as a side dish to game.

Quinces in spiced syrup

Makes 2 small preserving jars • **Prep** 10 mins • **Cooking** 1¼ hours

INGREDIENTS

900g (2lb) quinces, scrubbed

1 tbsp lemon juice

275g (9½oz) caster sugar

2 star anise, 1 cinnamon stick, or 2 cloves

METHOD

1 Place the quinces in a saucepan, add 600ml (1 pint) of water, bring to a boil, and simmer for 2 minutes. Remove the quinces from the pan and plunge them into cold water. Reserve the pan of water. Peel, core, and quarter the quinces and put into cold water with the lemon juice.

2 Stir the sugar into the reserved pan of water. Heat the pan gently until the sugar dissolves, then stir well. Drain the quince quarters and add them to the syrup along with the spices. Bring to a boil, reduce the heat, cover and poach gently for 12–15 minutes, or until just tender.

3 Preheat the oven to 150°C/300°F/Gas 2. Pack the quinces into the warm sterilized preserving jars, leaving 1cm (½in) space at the top. Bring the syrup back to a boil and pour over the fruit to cover it completely. Tap the jar gently on a wooden board to remove air bubbles. Fit the rubber band or metal lid seal, and clamp on the lid. If using screw-band jars, loosen by a quarter turn.

4 Place the jars on a baking tray lined with baking paper in the oven for 40–50 minutes. Remove, and tighten the clips or screw bands (fit plastic screw bands at this point).

Note Keeps for 12 months if heat-processed.

PLUMS

When to pick
Pick dessert plums when as ripe as possible, but still firm. They should come away from the branch easily. Cooking plums can be picked earlier if needed.

Eat and store fresh
Eat plums within a few days of picking, before they become too soft. If cooking, store for up to 5 days in the fridge before use.

How to preserve
Use plums in jams or savoury chutneys. You can also crystallize them or use them to make plum wine.

❄ **Freezing options**
Destone, cut in half, and open freeze. If using in jams and chutneys, freeze whole. They can also be poached in syrup and frozen (see pages 194–5).

This stunning dessert recipe is equally good when made with damsons or cherries, but instead of putting the marzipan in the fruit cavities, dot little pieces between each fruit.

Plum and marzipan
clafoutis

Serves 6 • Prep 30 mins • Cooking 50 mins

INGREDIENTS

For the marzipan
115g (4oz) ground almonds
60g (2oz) caster sugar
60g (2oz) icing sugar
a few drops of natural almond extract
1/2 tsp lemon juice
1 egg white, lightly beaten

For the clafoutis
675g (1 1/2 lb) plums, halved and stoned
75g (2 1/2 oz) butter
4 eggs and 1 egg yolk
115g (4oz) caster sugar, plus extra for dusting
85g (3oz) plain flour, sifted
450ml (15fl oz) milk
150ml (5fl oz) single cream

METHOD

1 Mix the marzipan ingredients together with enough of the egg white to form a stiff paste. Push a tiny piece of the paste into the cavity in each plum half.

2 Grease a shallow, ovenproof dish, large enough to hold the plums in a single layer, with 15g (1/2oz) of the butter. Arrange the plums cut-side down in the dish, with the marzipan underneath. Melt the remaining butter and leave to cool.

3 Preheat the oven to 190°C (375°F/Gas 5). Add any leftover egg white from the marzipan to the eggs and egg yolk. Add the sugar, and whisk until thick and pale. Whisk in the melted butter, the flour, milk, and cream to form a batter. Pour over the plums. Bake in the oven for about 50 minutes until golden and just set. Serve warm, dusted with caster sugar.

Note You can use shop-bought white marzipan for speed. Try serving with whipped cream, flavoured with a little sugar and grated orange zest.

Use up the contents of your autumn fruit bowl in this delicious, easy-to-make dessert. Even more mouthwatering when served with crème fraîche or ice cream.

Caramelized autumn
fruit pudding

Serves 6 • **Prep** 10 mins • **Cooking** 20 mins

INGREDIENTS

3 Granny Smith apples, peeled, cored, and quartered

3 firm Conference pears, peeled, cored, and quartered

4 firm red plums, quartered and stoned

60g (2oz) butter

60g (2oz) caster sugar

2 tbsp orange juice or water

METHOD

1 To make the caramel, heat the butter in a large frying pan over medium heat. Add the sugar and orange juice and cook, stirring, until the sugar dissolves. Increase the heat and boil until the mixture turns golden brown.

2 Add the apples and cook gently, stirring, until they start to soften, then add the pears and cook until soft.

3 Add the plums and continue to cook, stirring occasionally, until all the fruit is softened, but not falling apart, and is coated in caramel. Serve warm.

Variation You could also make this with summer fruits, such as apricots, peaches, and blackberries.

The addition of port and cinnamon turns this simple plum jam into something special, with more than a hint of festive flavours. In a pretty glass jar this would make an ideal Christmas gift.

Spiced port
and plum jam

Makes approx. 2kg (4¹/₂lb) or 6 medium jars • **Prep** 15 mins • **Cooking** 20–28 mins

INGREDIENTS

1.8kg (4lb) dark plums,
   halved and stoned
1 cinnamon stick,
   snapped in half
juice of 1 lime
1.35kg (3lb) sugar
2–3 tbsp port (to taste)

METHOD

1 Put the plums, cinnamon stick, and lime juice into a preserving pan or a large heavy saucepan, then pour over 600ml (1 pint) of water.

2 Simmer gently on low heat for 15–20 minutes or until the plums begin to break down and soften.

3 Add the sugar, stir until it has all dissolved, then bring to a boil and keep at a rolling boil for 5–8 minutes or until the jam begins to thicken and reaches the setting point. Remove the pan from the heat while you test for a set (see pages 186–7).

4 Discard the cinnamon stick, stir in the port, then ladle into warm sterilized jars, cover with waxed paper discs, seal, and label.

Note Store in a cool, dark place, and refrigerate after opening. Keeps for 9 months unopened.

Make chutney

Chutneys are versatile sweet-sour mixtures of vegetables, fruit, spices, and dried fruits, cooked until soft. They are usually eaten with cold meats and cheese. This recipe shows the basic method, which can be made with all kinds of seasonal produce. For the best chutney, always prepare ingredients carefully to achieve the desired texture. Ideally, grind your own spices for the freshest flavour, and cook the chutney slowly and gently, stirring often to prevent the mixture burning on the base of the pan.

1 **Prepare the fruit** Put all the ingredients into a preserving pan or large heavy saucepan and bring to a boil slowly, stirring to dissolve the sugar.

2 **Simmer and stir** Simmer gently for $1\frac{1}{2}$–2 hours until a wooden spoon drawn across the base of the pan leaves a trail. Stir frequently towards the end.

Recipe Plum chutney

Makes approx. 1.35kg (3lb) or 3 large jars
Prep 1 hour 50 mins–2 hours • **Keeps** 12 months

INGREDIENTS

1kg (2^1/$_4$lb) plums, halved, destoned, quartered

350g (12oz) cooking apples, cored, peeled, diced

250g (9oz) onions, sliced

300g (10^1/$_2$oz) light soft brown sugar

125g (4^1/$_2$oz) raisins

1 tsp sea salt

1 tsp each allspice, cinnamon, and coriander

^{1}/$_2$ tsp dried chilli flakes

600ml (1 pint) white wine or cider vinegar

Best fruit and vegetables for chutney

There are endless combinations of ingredients that can be used in chutneys.

Apples A key fruit for chutneys as its flavour blends well with other ingredients.
Onions Essential for all chutneys. Try red or white onions, and shallots for a milder flavour.
Pears Combine with fresh ginger or spices such as cardamom, cinnamon, allspice.
Peppers These add sweetness and colour.
Plums Add for rich chutneys with lots of body.
Rhubarb Use tender, less fibrous stems.

3 **Put into jars** The chutney should now look thick and glossy. Check the seasoning, add more salt if necessary, and pot into warm sterilized jars, leaving no air gaps.

4 **Cover and store** Cover with waxed paper, seal, label, and store in a cool, dark place. Leave to mature and mellow for at least 1–2 months before using.

FIGS

When to pick
Pick figs when they are fully coloured and slightly soft. Sticky nectar oozing out of one end is an indicator of ripeness. Figs for cooking may be picked earlier.

Eat and store fresh
Eat figs raw within a couple of days of picking. Less ripe figs can be stored in the fridge and used in cooking up to 5 days after harvesting.

How to preserve
Figs can be used in jams, chutneys, and pickles, as well as being bottled or dried.

Chargrilling figs seems to enhance their rich flavour. The addition of a creamy blue cheese, such as Gorgonzola, gives a welcome contrast to the natural sweetness of the figs and honey.

Chargrilled figs
with Gorgonzola and honey

Serves 4 • **Prep** 10 mins • **Cooking** 10 mins

INGREDIENTS

12 ripe figs, halved

175g (6oz) Gorgonzola
    cheese, crumbled

clear honey, to serve

METHOD

1 Heat a ridged grill pan over medium-high heat. Add the figs, placing them cut-side down, and grill for 5 minutes, or until browned.

2 When the figs have nice grill marks, gently turn them over and cook on the other side for a further couple of minutes.

3 Remove the figs from the pan and place them in a shallow serving dish. Sprinkle with the Gorgonzola, drizzle with honey, and serve immediately.

Note These are good with pre-dinner drinks, or served at the end of a meal.

A richly dense, fruity jam like this can be served with sweet or savoury food. For a spicier alternative, add a couple of teaspoons of chopped, crystallized ginger to the figs as they cook.

Ripe fig
and vanilla jam

Makes approx. 1.1kg (2¹/₂lb) or 3 medium jars • **Prep** 10 mins • **Cooking** 40–45 mins

INGREDIENTS

675g (1¹/₂lb) ripe figs with soft skins, topped and tailed, and cut into quarters

zest and juice of 1 lemon

1 small cooking apple, peeled, cored, and roughly chopped

1 vanilla pod, sliced lengthways

675g (1¹/₂lb) caster or granulated sugar

METHOD

1 Put the figs in a preserving pan or a large heavy saucepan with the lemon zest and juice, chopped apple, and vanilla pod. Cook on low heat for about 20 minutes or so, stirring occasionally, until the figs have softened and broken down.

2 Add the sugar and cook on low heat, stirring continuously, until all the sugar has dissolved. Then bring to a boil and cook at a rolling boil, stirring occasionally, for about 15–20 minutes or until it reaches the setting point. Skim away any scum as it cooks. Remove the pan from the heat while you test for a set (see pages 186–7).

3 Carefully remove the vanilla pod, then ladle into warm sterilized jars, cover with discs of waxed paper, seal, and label.

Note Store in a cool, dark place, and refrigerate after opening. Keeps for 6 months unopened.

WINTER

Broccoli

Brussels sprouts

Oriental greens

Kale

Cabbages

Leeks

Chicory

Celeriac

Jerusalem artichokes

Swedes

Turnips

Parsnips

BROCCOLI

When to pick
Harvest the central flower head when it is no bigger than your hand, and the buds are tight. Do not leave until the flowers open. Side shoots can be cooked as individual spears.

Eat and store fresh
Broccoli can be stored in a cool place or in the fridge for up to 5 days. Eat before yellowing appears.

Freezing options
Wash, divide into florets, blanch for 2 minutes, cool, and freeze for up to 12 months.

In Italy, this warm, garlicky dip is traditionally served with raw vegetables, like baby carrots and radishes, but I have found it is perfect with lightly steamed sprouting broccoli.

Steamed broccoli
with bagna càuda

Serves 4, makes about 150ml (5fl oz) dipping sauce • **Prep** 10 mins • **Cooking** 10 mins

INGREDIENTS

500g (1lb 2oz) purple sprouting or young broccoli spears, trimmed
4 chopped anchovies
2 garlic cloves, crushed
100ml (3½fl oz) extra virgin olive oil
25g (scant 1oz) cold butter
1 tsp lemon juice
sea salt and freshly ground black pepper

METHOD

1 Steam the broccoli for no more than 5 minutes until it is just *al dente*.

2 Put the anchovies into a mortar and pestle, and grind them to a paste. Put them in a small saucepan along with the garlic and oil, and heat gently for 2 minutes until the garlic is lightly coloured, but not brown.

3 Remove the pan from the heat and use a wire whisk to add the cold butter in small pieces, beating well between additions.

4 Add the lemon juice and continue to whisk until the mixture emulsifies slightly, then season to taste. Serve the dipping sauce warm with the broccoli.

Here is a quick and simple way to make the most of your delicious young sprouting broccoli. The spicy chilli and zesty lemon flavours are perfect for the winter months.

Spicy spaghetti
with sprouting broccoli

Serves 4 • **Prep** 5 mins • **Cooking** 20 mins

INGREDIENTS

200g (7oz) white or purple sprouting broccoli
400g (14oz) dried spaghetti
extra virgin olive oil, for frying
bunch of spring onions, chopped
1/2 tsp dried chilli flakes
juice of 1/2 lemon
sea salt and freshly ground black pepper
25g (scant 1oz) Parmesan cheese, or hard sheep's cheese, grated

METHOD

1 Trim the sprouting broccoli and separate any multiple florets into single heads so that all are similar sized for even cooking. Slice any thicker stems in half and others diagonally.

2 Cook the spaghetti in a large pan of boiling salted water until *al dente*. Drain and return to the pan.

3 Meanwhile, heat the olive oil in a non-stick wok or large frying pan, then add the sprouting broccoli and spring onions and cook over medium heat for 5–10 minutes or until tender.

4 Tip the broccoli into the pan with the spaghetti. Add the chilli flakes, lemon juice, and season with salt and pepper to taste. Toss lightly over gentle heat. Serve immediately with a sprinkling of the Parmesan or hard sheep's cheese.

In this tasty supper dish, the broccoli is cooked for slightly longer than usual and then mashed. The addition of lemon and chilli really lifts the flavours of this common brassica.

Marinated lamb chops
with chilli broccoli

Serves 4 • **Prep** 5 mins, plus marinating • **Cooking** 30 mins

INGREDIENTS

4 lean lamb loin chops,
    fat removed
sea salt and freshly ground
    black pepper
handful of rosemary sprigs
300g (10^{1}/$_{2}$oz) broccoli florets
    and stalks chopped
    fairly small
juice of 1 lemon
pinch of chilli flakes
mint jelly, to serve

For the marinade

2 tbsp sherry vinegar, cider
    vinegar, or white
    wine vinegar
pinch of caster sugar
splash of dark soy sauce

METHOD

1 Preheat the oven to 200°C (400°F/Gas 6). First, prepare the marinade. Mix together the vinegar, sugar, and soy sauce, then pour over the lamb. Leave to marinate for 5 minutes, or longer if time permits.

2 Sit the lamb chops in a roasting tin, season well with salt and black pepper, and throw in the rosemary sprigs. Roast in the oven for 20–30 minutes until cooked to your liking.

3 While the lamb is cooking, put the broccoli in a pan of boiling salted water, and cook for about 10 minutes until just soft. Drain, keeping the broccoli in the pan, then mash very gently with a fork. Squeeze over the lemon juice, and add the chilli, a pinch of salt, and some black pepper. Put a lid on the pan, and give it a shake. Serve immediately with the roasted lamb chops and mint jelly on the side.

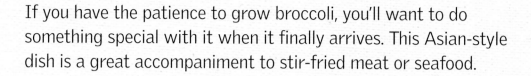

If you have the patience to grow broccoli, you'll want to do something special with it when it finally arrives. This Asian-style dish is a great accompaniment to stir-fried meat or seafood.

Stir-fried broccoli
with sesame seeds

Serves 4 • **Prep** 5 mins • **Cooking** 6 mins

INGREDIENTS

1 tbsp sesame seeds

1 tbsp vegetable oil

1 tbsp light soy sauce

pinch of dried chilli flakes

675g (1½lb) broccoli, florets and stems

60ml (2fl oz) vegetable stock or water

sea salt and freshly ground black pepper

METHOD

1 Heat a large non-stick frying pan or wok. Add the sesame seeds and toast them, shaking the pan constantly for 1–2 minutes, or until the seeds turn golden. Transfer to a plate.

2 Add the oil, soy sauce, and chilli flakes to the pan, and stir to combine. Add the broccoli and stir-fry for 2 minutes.

3 Pour in the stock and cover the pan. Cook for 1–2 minutes, or until the broccoli is tender but still crisp. Stir in the sesame seeds and season to taste with salt and pepper before serving.

BRUSSELS SPROUTS

When to pick
Harvest these tiny brassicas from the bottom of the plant upwards, when they are no bigger than a walnut, and the leaves are tight and firm. Pick as required, leaving the upper buds to mature on the plant.

Eat and store fresh
Shred and eat tiny sprouts raw. Store larger ones in the fridge for 3–5 days. To prepare, peel the outer leaves and cut a cross in the base to allow equal cooking of the stem and leaves.

Freezing options
Trim and blanch for 2–3 minutes, cool, and freeze for up to 12 months.

Although many people dislike Brussels sprouts, it is hard to find someone who doesn't like them when treated in this manner. A perfect foil to a Thanksgiving or Christmas meal.

Brussels sprouts with chestnuts and pancetta

Serves 4 • Prep 10 mins • Cooking 10 mins

INGREDIENTS

400g (14oz) Brussels sprouts, washed and trimmed
100g (3½oz) pancetta, diced
knob of butter
100g (3½oz) chestnuts, cooked, peeled, and roughly chopped
1 tsp grated lemon zest
sea salt and freshly ground black pepper

METHOD

1 Boil the Brussels sprouts in plenty of salted water for 5–7 minutes, depending on their size, until they are just tender, but not overcooked. Drain them well.

2 In a large frying pan or wok, fry the pancetta in the butter for 3–4 minutes until crispy. Add the Brussels sprouts, chestnuts, and lemon zest, and continue to cook for 2 minutes until everything is heated through.

3 Season well with black pepper and a little salt, to taste; you may not need much as the pancetta can be very salty.

ORIENTAL GREENS

When to pick
Pick Asian leaves small for eating raw in salads, or leave to grow a little larger for stir fries. With spicy varieties, the larger the leaves, the hotter they will taste. Pick pak choi when the base bulb is swollen and firm.

Eat and store fresh
Eat baby leaves as soon as possible after picking if using raw. Wash and dry larger leaves, and store in a plastic bag in the fridge for up to 2 days. Store pak choi whole.

Freezing options
Blanch leaves for 1–2 minutes, cool, then freeze in freezer pots or bags. Depending on the greens, you may need to separate stalks from leaves and blanch stalks separately, for longer. Keeps for 9 months.

A selection of the finest greens your allotment has to offer can be used to make this recipe. Try any combination of oriental greens, spinach, chard, green beans, peas, or spring onions.

Oriental greens
with chilli, garlic, and soy

Serves 4 • Prep 15 mins • Cooking 15 mins

INGREDIENTS

handful of hazelnuts
1 tbsp sesame oil, or
    vegetable oil
2 medium-hot green chillies,
    deseeded and
    finely chopped
3 garlic cloves, thinly sliced
1 tbsp dark soy sauce
1 tbsp Chinese rice wine
1–2 heads pak choi,
    quartered lengthways
handful of spinach, or chard
2 handfuls of sugarsnap
    peas, or mangetout,
    sliced into strips
salt and freshly ground
    black pepper

METHOD

1 Spread the hazelnuts over a baking tray. Toast under a hot grill until golden brown, turning them frequently. Put the hazelnuts in a clean tea towel, and rub off the skins. Roughly chop, and set aside.

2 Heat the oil in a wok over medium-high heat, and swirl it around to coat the surface. Add the chillies and garlic, and cook for 10 seconds, then add the soy sauce and Chinese rice wine, and cook for a few seconds more.

3 Throw in the pak choi, and spinach or chard, and stir-fry for a minute. Add the sugarsnap peas or mangetout, and stir-fry for a minute more. Toss, and season with salt and black pepper. Serve immediately with the hazelnuts scattered over the top.

Oriental greens are easy to grow and provide a good source of dark green leafy vegetables in the winter. Try them stir-fried with Asian aromatics served with five-spice chicken.

Spicy honeyed chicken
with chilli greens

Serves 4 • **Prep** 10 mins • **Cooking** 45 mins, plus marinating

INGREDIENTS

2 handfuls of Chinese greens,
    such as pak choi, sliced

splash of light soy sauce

2.5cm (1in) piece of root
    ginger, grated

pinch of chilli flakes

salt and freshly ground
    black pepper

1–2 tbsp clear honey

juice of 2 limes

3 tbsp extra virgin olive oil

2 tbsp five-spice powder, or
    1 tsp five-spice powder mixed
    with 1 tbsp sesame oil

8 chicken pieces (a mixture
    of thighs and drumsticks),
    skin on

METHOD

1 Preheat the oven to 200°C (400°F/Gas 6). Put the greens in a large bowl. Add the soy sauce, ginger, and chilli flakes, and season well. Set aside.

2 In another bowl, mix together the honey, lime juice, 1 tablespoon of the oil, and the five-spice paste, until well combined. Spread over the chicken, and season well. Cover and leave to marinate in the fridge for at least 20 minutes.

3 Heat another tablespoon of the oil in a large frying pan over medium-high heat. Add the chicken pieces, skin-side down, and cook a few pieces at a time if the pan is not big enough. Cook for 5–8 minutes on each side until golden and crispy, then transfer to a roasting tin. Roast in the oven for about 40 minutes until beginning to char.

4 Meanwhile, wipe the frying pan with kitchen paper, reduce the heat slightly, and add the greens. Drizzle over the remaining tablespoon of oil, and stir-fry for about 5 minutes until beginning to wilt. Serve hot with the crispy-skinned chicken.

This Asian-inspired recipe is a quick yet luxurious way to serve beef with pak choi from your allotment. It is important to use the best quality meat you can, as it is simply spiced and cooked.

Wasabi beef
with pak choi

Serves 4 • **Prep** 10 mins • **Cooking** 10 mins

INGREDIENTS

2 tbsp extra virgin olive oil

2 tsp wasabi paste

4 sirloin steaks, about
   200g (7oz) each

200g (7oz) pak choi, cut
   lengthways into 8 pieces

5 garlic cloves, grated or
   finely chopped

1 tbsp dark soy sauce

salt and freshly ground
   black pepper

METHOD

1 Heat a ridged grill pan until hot. Mix 1 tablespoon of the olive oil with the wasabi paste. Use to coat the sirloin steaks, ensuring a thin, even covering.

2 Add the steaks to the griddle pan and cook fiercely over high heat for 3 minutes on each side. Remove to a plate, and leave to rest in a warm place for 5 minutes.

3 Meanwhile, toss the pak choi in the remaining olive oil with the garlic and soy sauce. Cook in the griddle pan for 2–3 minutes, or until charred and just wilted. To serve, cut the steak into 1cm ($^1/_2$in) slices, season, and serve with the pak choi.

Note This can also be cooked on a barbecue or charcoal grill.

Oriental greens are perfect in stir-fries, adding colour and a fresh flavour to the finished dish. The rice noodles used here are quite delicate, so be careful not to overcook them.

Thai noodle stir-fry

Serves 4 • **Prep** 15 mins • **Cooking** 20 mins

INGREDIENTS

175g (6oz) thin rice noodles

1 stalk of lemongrass, outer leaves removed, woody end trimmed, and finely chopped

3 tbsp groundnut oil or vegetable oil

3 skinless boneless chicken breasts, cut into thin strips

1 onion, sliced

1 tsp finely grated root ginger

1 red chilli, deseeded and finely chopped

1 orange pepper, deseeded and sliced

115g (4oz) shiitake mushrooms, sliced

2 heads of pak choi, shredded

2 tbsp light soy sauce

1 tbsp Thai fish sauce

1 tsp sweet chilli sauce

METHOD

1 Soak the noodles in a bowl of boiling water until softened, or as directed on the packet. Drain and set aside.

2 Heat 2 tbsp of the oil in a wok and stir-fry the chicken over a high heat for 2–3 minutes, or until lightly browned. Remove from the pan and set aside.

3 Reduce the heat to medium, add the remaining oil, and stir-fry the onion for 2 minutes. Add the lemongrass, ginger, chilli, orange pepper, and mushrooms, and stir-fry for 2 minutes.

4 Add the pak choi and stir-fry for a further 2 minutes, then return the chicken to the pan and add the noodles. Pour in the soy sauce, fish sauce, and sweet chilli sauce, and toss everything together over the heat for 2–3 minutes, or until piping hot and the chicken is cooked through. Serve at once.

Cavolo nero, or Tuscan kale, is an extremely tasty, dark leafed kale and one of the hardiest sources of greens in the allotment. Its strong flavours work well with smoked fish and garlic.

Portuguese-style kale
and haddock soup

Serves 4 • **Prep** 20 mins • **Cooking** 20 mins

INGREDIENTS

2 tbsp extra virgin olive oil

1 onion, finely chopped

3 garlic cloves, peeled and crushed

1 large waxy potato, peeled and diced

250ml (8fl oz) full-fat or semi-skimmed milk

salt and freshly ground black pepper

300g (10oz) cavolo nero or kale, rinsed, ribs removed and finely shredded

300g (10oz) smoked haddock fillet, skinned and flaked

METHOD

1 Heat the oil in a sauté pan over medium heat, add the onion and garlic and stir for 4–5 minutes, until softened.

2 Add the potato and milk, then pour in enough water to cover everything by 2–3cm ($^3/_4$–1$^1/_4$in). Season generously, bring to a simmer and cook for 5 minutes, then add the cabbage and continue cooking for 10–15 minutes until the vegetables are tender.

3 Stir in the haddock and simmer for 1 minute, then take off the heat and cover. Leave to stand for 5 minutes before serving.

KALE

When to pick
Harvest this valuable source of winter greens as needed. Pick the biggest leaves first, leaving the smaller ones to mature on the plant, unless you want to eat them raw in salads.

Eat and store fresh
Eat the baby leaves raw. Trim the central rib out of larger leaves, as they can be a bit tough. Wash, dry, and store larger leaves in a plastic bag in the fridge for up to 3 days.

 Freezing options
Remove any tough stalks, slice, then blanch for 2 minutes and leave to cool before freezing in freezer pots or bags. Keeps for 6 months.

This extremely tasty and economical dish, based on a traditional Tuscan soup, is my Monday night supper. To make your own store of haricot beans, leave French beans to dry on the stalk.

Monday night "ribollita"

Serves 4 • **Prep** 10 mins, plus soaking • **Cooking** 2 hours 20 mins

INGREDIENTS

1 leftover roasted chicken carcass

2 sticks celery, 1 roughly chopped and 1 finely diced

2 carrots, 1 roughly chopped and 1 finely diced

2 small onions, 1 roughly chopped and 1 finely diced

1 bay leaf

1 bouquet garni

sea salt and freshly ground black pepper

100g (3½oz) dried haricot beans, soaked overnight

2 tbsp extra virgin olive oil

50g (1¾oz) pancetta, diced

2 garlic cloves, crushed

2 sprigs of thyme

2 handfuls or 100g (3½oz) kale, shredded

25g (scant 1oz) Parmesan cheese, grated

METHOD

1 Put the chicken carcass and roughly chopped celery, carrot, and onion into a large saucepan, along with the bay leaf, bouquet garni, seasoning, and 3 litres (5¼ pints) water. Bring to the boil and simmer for 1½ hours until the carcass has broken down completely. Strain the stock into another pan, reserving the carcass until cool enough to handle, then prise out all the bits of cooked meat and add them back to the stock. Clean the pan and return it to the hob.

2 Meanwhile, rinse the soaked beans and place in a pan with plenty of cold water. Bring to the boil, skim the top, and turn down the heat to a simmer. Cook the beans for about 1 hour, until softened. Drain and set aside.

3 Heat the olive oil in the large saucepan and add the pancetta. Cook for 2–3 minutes on medium heat, until crispy. Add the diced onion, carrot, and celery. Then add the garlic and thyme. Continue to cook for a further 2–3 minutes, until the vegetables are soft. Pour in the chicken stock and add the drained beans. Simmer the stew for 30–40 minutes, uncovered, until the beans are very soft.

4 Add the kale, cover, and cook for 5 minutes until wilted. Season to taste, add the Parmesan, and serve with bread.

CABBAGES

When to pick

Pick cabbages when the heads are tight, firm, and heavy for their size. Winter cabbages are frost hardy, so they can be left on the plant and harvested as needed.

Eat and store fresh

Eat young fresh cabbage raw in salads and coleslaws. Store large cabbages in a cool, dark place for several weeks, or in the fridge for up to 1 week.

How to preserve

Cabbage is often used in relishes and pickles and can be salted to make sauerkraut (see pages 330–1).

Freezing options

Wash, chop, and blanch for 2 minutes. Then cool and freeze for up to 6 months.

A traditional country soup, this dish takes minutes to prepare and makes a substantial lunch or supper, served alongside some fresh crusty bread. For a vegetarian option leave out the lardons.

French cabbage soup

Serves 4 • Prep 15 mins • Cooking 30 mins

INGREDIENTS

1 tbsp extra virgin olive oil
100g (3^1/$_2$oz) lardons, or diced bacon
1 Spanish onion, finely chopped
1 garlic clove, crushed
1 large Savoy cabbage, halved, core discarded, and leaves cut into shreds
sea salt and freshly ground black pepper
3 sprigs of parsley

METHOD

1 Heat the oil in a casserole over medium heat. Add the lardons (setting aside 2 tbsp to finish), onion, and garlic. Fry, stirring frequently, for 3–4 minutes or until the onion and garlic start to colour. Add the cabbage shreds, reserving a handful to finish. Stir well and season lightly with sea salt, and generously with pepper. Continue frying for 2–3 minutes, stirring occasionally.

2 Add 850ml (1^1/$_2$ pints) boiling water over the vegetables and lardons, stir well, and add the parsley. Cover, lower the heat a little, and simmer gently for about 20 minutes, stirring occasionally.

3 Meanwhile, place a non-stick frying pan over medium heat. Add the reserved lardons and fry until crisp and golden. Then add the reserved cabbage shreds and fry them until they have wilted, stirring frequently. Season with a little pepper.

4 Taste the soup and adjust the seasoning. Lift out the parsley. Ladle into 4 bowls and scatter over the fried bacon and cabbage mixture.

Note The soup will freeze for up to 3 months without the lardon garnish.

This is a simpler version of the Thai salad *som tam*, which has a wonderful sweet and sour, salty, and hot dressing. Eat it just as it is, or add some cooled rice noodles to turn it into a main course.

Thai vegetable salad
with cabbage and peanuts

Serves 4 • **Prep** 15 mins

INGREDIENTS

2 dessert apples

4 carrots, peeled and grated

1 small white cabbage, shredded

handful of sunflower seeds

handful of salted, or
    dry-roasted peanuts

For the dressing

1 tbsp light soy sauce

1 tbsp Thai fish sauce, such
    as nam pla

1 green chilli, deseeded and
    finely chopped

1 garlic clove, grated

juice of 2 limes

1–2 tsp caster sugar

handful of coriander,
    finely chopped

salt and freshly ground
    black pepper

METHOD

1 First, make the dressing. Put all the dressing ingredients in a small bowl, and mix thoroughly until the sugar has dissolved. Taste, and season with salt and black pepper as needed, then check the seasoning again. If it needs sweetening, add more sugar, and if it needs saltiness, add a little more fish sauce.

2 Quarter and core the apples, then chop into bite-sized pieces. Put in a bowl with the carrot, cabbage, and sunflower seeds. Toss well. Drizzle over the dressing, and toss together so that everything is well mixed. Transfer to a serving dish, and scatter over the peanuts.

In this dish, the slow braising of the guinea fowl allows the tender cabbage to soak up the rich flavours of the stock, transforming the humble Savoy into something really special.

Pot-roasted guinea fowl
with cabbage and walnuts

Serves 4 • **Prep** 20 mins • **Cooking** 1 hour

INGREDIENTS

2 guinea fowls, about
1.25kg (2¾lb) each
salt and freshly ground
black pepper
30g (1oz) butter
2 tbsp extra virgin olive oil
1 small onion, finely chopped
1 leek, thinly sliced
2 celery sticks, sliced
100g (3½oz) smoked streaky
bacon rashers, diced
85g (3oz) walnuts, halved
1 small Savoy cabbage,
about 400g (14oz)
100ml (3½fl oz) hot
chicken stock

METHOD

1 Preheat the oven to 200°C (400°F/Gas 6). Season the guinea fowls with salt and pepper.

2 Heat the butter with half the oil in a large, deep, flameproof casserole, and fry the guinea fowls on medium heat for 10 minutes, turning to brown on all sides. Remove from the heat and lift out the birds.

3 Add the remaining oil to the casserole with the onion, leek, celery, and bacon, and fry, stirring, for 2–3 minutes, or until lightly coloured. Add the walnuts, then place the guinea fowl back on top of the fried vegetables.

4 Cut the cabbage into 8 wedges. Tuck them into the casserole. Pour over the hot stock and season lightly. Bring to a boil, then cover and cook in the preheated oven for 45 minutes, or until the vegetables are tender and the guinea fowl juices run clear when pierced with a skewer.

5 Leave to stand for 10 minutes before serving. To serve, remove the guinea fowls and cut each one in half. Arrange on plates and serve with vegetables and stock.

This traditional Christmas recipe belonged to my great and great-great grandmothers, a cheroot-smoking, poker-playing mother and daughter team who ran a restaurant in southern Sweden.

Slow-cooked Swedish
red cabbage

Serves 8 as a side dish • **Prep** 20 mins • **Cooking** 2 hours 20 mins

INGREDIENTS

50g (1³/₄oz) butter

25g (scant 1oz) caster sugar

1 tsp salt

6 tbsp rice wine vinegar, or
   white wine or cider vinegar

1 red cabbage approx. 1kg
   (2¹/₄lb), finely shredded

2 apples, peeled, cored,
   and grated

2 heaped tbsp redcurrant jelly

METHOD

1 Preheat the oven to 150°C (300°F/Gas 2). In a large, heavy flameproof casserole, heat together the butter, sugar, salt, 6 tablespoons of water, and vinegar. Bring to a boil and simmer for 1 minute.

2 Fold the cabbage into the liquid and bring it back to a boil. Take the casserole off the heat and cover tightly with a double layer of foil. Fit the lid on snugly and cook in the oven for 1¹/₂ hours.

3 Remove from the oven and add the grated apples and redcurrant jelly, stirring well. Add a little more water if it looks dry. Replace the foil and the lid, and return the cabbage to the oven for a further 30 minutes. Serve warm.

LEEKS

When to pick
Pick leeks young for a more delicate flavour. Larger leeks should be harvested when tall and firm, and before the centre starts to harden and bolt.

Eat and store fresh
Eat baby leeks within 2 days of picking. Leave larger leeks in the ground until needed, and then store cleaned but untrimmed in the fridge for up to 1 week.

How to preserve
Leeks can be used in chutneys and pickles. Baby leeks can be chargrilled and preserved in oil (see pages 38–9).

Alliums are not often used as a main ingredient, but they sometimes deserve to be given a starring role. Served like this, baby leeks make a delicious starter or side dish.

Roasted baby leeks
with tomato dressing

Serves 4 • Prep 10 mins • Cooking 12 mins

INGREDIENTS

1 tbsp finely chopped sun-dried tomatoes in oil

3 tbsp extra virgin olive oil, plus extra for tossing

1 tbsp red wine vinegar

1 tbsp very finely chopped black and green olives

1 tbsp finely chopped basil

sea salt and freshly ground black pepper

8 baby leeks, washed and trimmed

METHOD

1 Preheat the oven to 200°C (400°F/Gas 6). In a bowl, mix the tomatoes with a little of their oil, the olive oil, vinegar, olives, and basil. Season to taste.

2 Put the leeks in a pan of boiling water and cook over high heat for 2 minutes. Drain well.

3 Toss a little olive oil in a roasting tin and place the leeks in the tin. Roast in the oven for 10 minutes until golden and tender. Spoon the dressing over to serve.

This is an easy way to make soup, using a potato masher rather than a blender to reduce the cooked potatoes to a rough purée. The finished soup has an interesting texture and hearty flavour.

Leek and potato soup

Serves 4 • **Prep** 15–20 mins • **Cooking** 1 hour

INGREDIENTS

1kg (2^1/$_4$lb) potatoes, peeled
   but left whole
500g (1lb 2oz) leeks, washed,
   trimmed, and shredded
1 large onion, chopped
1.5 litres (2^3/$_4$ pints)
   vegetable stock
50g (1^3/$_4$oz) butter
salt and freshly ground
   black pepper

METHOD

1 Put the potatoes, leeks, onion, and stock in a large pan. Season lightly. Bring to a boil, reduce the heat, cover, and simmer for 30 minutes.

2 Using a slotted spoon, lift the potatoes out of the pan and mash with the butter. Return the mashed potatoes to the pan, stir thoroughly, and simmer for a further 25–30 minutes, stirring occasionally. If the soup gets too thick, simply add a little extra water to thin down to the required consistency. Taste and season again with salt, if necessary. Ladle into warm bowls and add a good grinding of pepper to serve.

When to pick
Harvest chicory when young to eat raw in salads. Leave to grow larger for cooking.

Eat and store fresh
Eat salad varieties as soon as possible, or store in the fridge, unwashed, for up to 3 days. Eat radicchio raw, or chargrilled with pasta dishes. Endives can be cooked or eaten raw.

This elegant soup is best served well chilled. The subtle flavour of white chicory combines perfectly with orange to make a delicate and refreshing start to a meal.

Chicory gazpacho

Serves 4 • **Prep** 15 mins, plus chilling

INGREDIENTS

1 large orange
2 heads white chicory
   (Belgian endive)
2 slices bread, crusts removed
1 garlic clove, roughly chopped
4 spring onions, trimmed and
   roughly chopped
1 large beefsteak tomato,
   skinned, quartered,
   and deseeded
450ml (15fl oz) cold
   vegetable stock
2 tbsp extra virgin olive oil,
   plus extra for garnish
2 tbsp white balsamic
   condiment
4 large basil leaves
salt and freshly ground
   black pepper

METHOD

1 Thinly pare the zest of half the orange. Cut in thin strips and boil in water for 1 minute. Drain, rinse with cold water, and drain again. Set aside for garnish. Finely grate the zest from the remaining half of the orange, squeeze the juice, and set aside.

2 Cut a cone shape out of the base of each head of chicory and discard. Separate the heads into spears. Reserve 4 of the smallest spears for the garnish. Roughly chop the remainder.

3 Soak the bread in water for 2 minutes. Squeeze out some of the moisture, then put the bread in a blender with the chopped chicory, garlic, spring onions, tomato, stock, olive oil, white balsamic condiment, basil leaves, and the orange juice and finely grated zest. Purée the soup in a blender or food processor then season to taste. Chill until ready to serve.

4 Ladle into 4 shallow soup plates, and drizzle with a little olive oil. Garnish each with a tiny chicory spear and a few strands of blanched orange zest. Serve cold.

Note The soup can be frozen for up to 3 months.

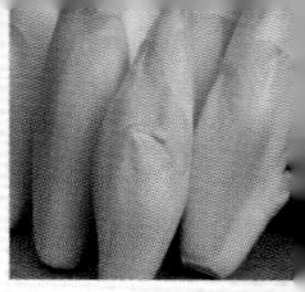

The slight bitterness of the chicory in this salad works well with the sweetness of the pears and the strong mustard dressing. This would be delicious served with a barbecued fillet of beef.

Chicory salad
with spinach and pears

Serves 6 • **Prep** 10 mins

INGREDIENTS

200g (7oz) baby spinach leaves
2 heads white chicory
   (Belgian endive), core
   removed and leaves
   separated
2 firm, ripe pears,
   peeled and sliced
3 shallots, finely sliced

For the vinaigrette

1 tbsp clear honey
$1/2$ tbsp Dijon mustard
6 tbsp extra virgin olive oil
2 tbsp red wine vinegar
salt and freshly ground
   black pepper

METHOD

1 To make the vinaigrette, place the honey, mustard, oil, and vinegar in a screw-top jar and shake well. Season to taste with salt and pepper. Alternatively, whisk the ingredients together in a bowl.

2 Place the spinach, chicory, sliced pears, and shallots in a salad bowl. Drizzle the vinaigrette over the salad, gently toss, and serve.

When to pick

Harvest these knobbly roots when they reach the size of a tennis ball or bigger. Do not let them get too big, as they can become tough and woody.

Eat and store fresh

Store celeriac for 1 week unwashed in the bottom of the fridge. Alternatively, leave them in the soil until hard frosts appear, or store in the same way as potatoes (see pages 140–1).

How to preserve

Use celeriac in pickles or cooked and preserved in oil.

Freezing options

Griddle slices and open freeze on trays, or freeze as a cooked purée, for up to 9 months.

This classic French bistro dish is traditionally served with cold meats or fish. The light and tangy mustard dressing works well with the celeriac and the dish is a good alternative to coleslaw.

Celeriac remoulade

Serves 6 as a side dish • **Prep** 15 mins

INGREDIENTS

2 shallots, finely chopped

2 tbsp chopped parsley

2 tbsp chopped tarragon leaves

2 tbsp Dijon mustard

1 tbsp capers, rinsed, gently
    dried, and chopped

4 cornichons, chopped

5 tbsp mayonnaise

1 celeriac, approx. 500g
    (1lb 2oz), peeled

juice of 1 lemon

salt and freshly ground
    black pepper

METHOD

1 In a small bowl, mix together the first 7 ingredients and season to taste.

2 Coarsely grate the celeriac, add the lemon juice, and mix well so the celeriac is coated all over in the juice.

3 Add the mayonnaise mixture, then mix again. Adjust the seasoning and chill until required.

Celeriac combines the mild taste of celery with the texture of potato to produce the perfect vegetable for soup. Any white-rinded soft cheese could be used in place of Camembert.

Camembert and celeriac
soup with cranberry swirl

Serves 4 • **Prep** 10 mins • **Cooking** 25 mins

INGREDIENTS

knob of butter

1 onion, chopped

1/2 small celeriac, about 225g (8oz) prepared weight, peeled and roughly diced

450ml (15fl oz) chicken or vegetable stock

1 bouquet garni

salt and freshly ground black pepper

450ml (15fl oz) milk

115g (4oz) ripe Camembert cheese, diced

4 tbsp double cream

4 tsp cranberry sauce

4 tsp orange or cranberry juice

4 tsp sunflower oil

METHOD

1 Melt the butter in a saucepan. Add the onion and fry gently, stirring, for 2 minutes, or until softened but not browned. Add the celeriac, stock, bouquet garni, and a little seasoning. Bring to a boil, reduce the heat, cover and simmer gently for 15 minutes, or until the celeriac is tender. Remove and discard the bouquet garni.

2 Purée using a hand-held blender or by transferring to a food processor, adding the milk and cheese. Return the soup to the rinsed-out pan, stir in the cream and reheat gently, but do not boil. Taste and adjust the seasoning.

3 Meanwhile, whisk the cranberry sauce with the juice and oil until thoroughly blended. Ladle the soup into warm, shallow soup plates. Whisk the cranberry mixture again and, using a teaspoon, swirl a little of the cranberry mixture into the centre of each bowl and quickly draw a cocktail stick from the centre to the edge all round to form a Catherine wheel shape. Serve immediately.

A hearty, warming pie, which you could also make using parsnips or Jerusalem artichokes instead of celeriac. The deep, earthy flavours work particularly well with the wholemeal pastry.

Celeriac soufflé pie

Serves 4 • **Prep** 40 mins, plus chilling • **Cooking** 50 mins

INGREDIENTS

For the pastry

175g (6oz) wholemeal or
   spelt flour
a good pinch of salt
1 tbsp caraway seeds
75g (2¹/₂oz) cold butter, diced
85g (3oz) farmhouse Cheddar
   cheese, grated
1 egg, separated

For the filling

1 celeriac, about 450g (1lb),
   peeled and cut into chunks
60g (2oz) butter
4 tbsp milk
4 streaky bacon rashers, diced
2 eggs, separated
2 tbsp snipped chives
freshly ground black pepper

METHOD

1 Mix the flour and salt in a bowl. Add the caraway seeds. Rub in the butter until the mixture resembles breadcrumbs. Stir in the cheese. Mix 3 tbsp cold water with the egg yolk, and stir into the flour mixture to form a firm dough, adding more water if necessary. Knead gently on a lightly floured surface, then wrap and chill for at least 30 minutes.

2 Meanwhile, cook the celeriac in boiling, salted water until tender. Drain and return to the pan. Dry out briefly over gentle heat. Mash with the butter and milk. Dry-fry the bacon and add to the celeriac with any fat in the pan. Beat in the egg yolks and chives. Season well.

3 Preheat the oven to 200°C (400°F/Gas 6). Roll out the pastry and use to line a 20cm (8in) flan tin. Line with greaseproof paper, and fill with baking beans. Bake blind in the oven for 10 minutes. Remove the paper and beans and cook for a further 5 minutes. Remove from the oven.

4 Whisk the 3 egg whites until stiff. Mix 1 tbsp of the whites into the celeriac mixture. Fold in the remainder with a metal spoon. Spoon into the pastry case and bake for 25 minutes until risen, just set, and golden. Serve hot.

JERUSALEM ARTICHOKES

When to pick
Harvest once the foliage has died down. In colder months, leave in the ground and dig up as required. If the ground is liable to freeze, harvest and store in a clamp (see pages 140–1).

Eat and store fresh
Eat roasted or puréed, in stews, as soups, or in gratins. Keep for up to 1 week in the fridge.

Freezing options
Jerusalem artichokes can be frozen once they have been cooked and puréed (see page 342).

These flavoursome, nutty tubers seem to spring up everywhere once planted. They can be difficult to prepare, although new varieties with smoother surfaces make the process easier.

Jerusalem artichoke
soup with saffron and thyme

Serves 4–6 • **Prep** 15 mins • **Cooking** 35–45 mins

INGREDIENTS

2 tbsp virgin rapeseed oil
    or extra virgin olive oil, plus
    extra to garnish
2 medium onions, chopped
3 garlic cloves, chopped
350g (12oz) Jerusalem
    artichokes, scrubbed and
    roughly chopped
350g (12oz) carrots, scrubbed
    and roughly chopped
sea salt
1.2 litres (2 pints) hot
    vegetable stock
1 tbsp fresh thyme leaves, or
    1^{1}/$_{2}$ tsp dried thyme
large pinch (about 30 strands)
    of saffron
juice of ^{1}/$_{2}$ lemon
freshly ground black pepper

METHOD

1 Heat the oil in a large pan over medium heat, add the onions, and fry for 5–10 minutes or until soft and translucent. Add the garlic and fry for 30 seconds or until fragrant. Stir in the artichokes, carrots, and a little salt, then cover with a lid and sweat, stirring frequently, for 10–15 minutes or until the vegetables are softened.

2 Add the stock, thyme, and saffron, bring to a boil, then lower the heat to a simmer and cook for 20 minutes or until the vegetables are thoroughly soft.

3 Cool briefly, then purée until smooth using a hand-held blender or by transferring to a food processor. Stir in the lemon juice and season to taste with salt and pepper. Serve in warm bowls, with a drizzle of oil on top.

Making a purée is one of the best ways to store Jerusalem artichokes. This tastes sublime served with roasted meat or game, baked with eggs and cream, or thinned as a soup.

Jerusalem artichoke
freezer purée

Makes approx. 1kg (2¼lb) • **Prep** 10 mins • **Cooking** 30 mins

INGREDIENTS

1 tbsp lemon juice
1kg (2¼lb) Jerusalem
    artichokes
5 tbsp double cream
50g (1¾oz) butter
a splash of whole milk
salt and freshly ground
    black pepper
pinch of grated nutmeg

METHOD

1 Stir the lemon juice into a large bowl of cold water. Peel the artichokes as thinly as possible, or leave the skins on and just scrub the vegetables if you don't mind a discoloured purée. Cut into neat pieces and put immediately into the acidulated water.

2 Drain, place in a large saucepan, and cover with fresh water. Bring to a boil, reduce the heat slightly, and simmer for about 25 minutes or until really tender. Drain and return to the pan. Heat gently to dry out.

3 Put the artichokes through a potato ricer, purée with a hand blender, process in a food processor, or mash thoroughly with a potato masher. Beat in the cream, butter, and milk, and season to taste with salt, black pepper, and the nutmeg.

4 Leave to cool, then pack in small portion-sized freezer containers with lids, or plastic freezer bags. Seal, label, and freeze. Thaw before reheating.

Note Keeps for 6 months in the freezer unopened.

Home-grown swedes tend to be smaller and sweeter than shop-bought ones. This versatile vegetable purée is absolutely delicious and can be served in place of mashed potatoes.

Creamed swedes

Serves 4–5 • **Prep** 10 mins • **Cooking** 25 mins

INGREDIENTS

1.1kg (2½lb) swedes, peeled
    and cut into chunks
salt and freshly ground
    black pepper
60g (2oz) butter
2–3 tbsp double cream
pinch of grated nutmeg

METHOD

1 Place the swedes in a large saucepan. Add enough cold water to cover, and a pinch of salt. Bring to a boil, cover, reduce the heat, and simmer for 20 minutes, or until tender. Drain well.

2 Return the drained swedes to the saucepan and place over very low heat. Add the butter, mash well, then add the cream and grated nutmeg. Season to taste with salt and pepper, and mash again until the swede is smooth.

Note To save time when planning a big meal, this purée can be made up to 2 days in advance. Chill until required and reheat just before serving.

When to pick
Young swedes have a sweet taste and can be picked from tennis-ball size upwards. Swedes may be left in the soil to grow larger, although they can become woody.

Eat and store fresh
Eat smaller swedes soon after harvesting. Store larger ones in the fridge for 1 week, or in a clamp for longer (see pages 140–1).

Freezing options
Freeze as a cooked purée and keep for up to 9 months.

TURNIPS

When to pick
Early turnips are delicious when picked at golf ball size. Leave other varieties to grow larger and they will have a stronger taste, and can turn woody.

Eat and store fresh
Eat baby turnips quickly, larger ones store in the fridge for 1 week, or leave in the ground until the first frosts, or harvest and clamp (see pages 140–1).

How to preserve
Turnips can be used in pickles and chutneys.

Freezing options
Freeze as a cooked purée and keep for up to 9 months.

Turnips are often overlooked, but you won't be disappointed with this light, colourful soup with a chilli kick. Larger turnips have a stronger flavour and are perfect for using in this recipe.

Turnip noodle soup
with pimento and chilli

Serves 4–6 • Prep 10 mins • Cooking 30 mins

INGREDIENTS

4 spring onions, chopped
2 good sized turnips, diced
1/2 tsp crushed dried chillies
1 green jalapeño chilli,
    deseeded and cut
    into thin rings
2 star anise
2 tsp tomato purée
900ml (1 1/2 pints) hot
    vegetable stock, or light
    chicken stock
1 slab dried, thin Chinese
    egg noodles
1 preserved pimento,
    drained and diced
soy sauce, to taste
freshly ground black pepper
small handful of coriander
    leaves, torn

METHOD

1 Put the spring onions, turnips, chillies, star anise, tomato purée, and stock in a saucepan and bring to a boil. Lower the heat, part-cover, and simmer gently for 30 minutes or until the turnips are really tender. Discard the star anise.

2 Meanwhile, put the noodles in a bowl, cover with boiling water, and leave to stand for 5 minutes, stirring to loosen, then drain. Stir the noodles into the soup, along with the pimento. Season to taste with soy sauce and pepper, then stir in half the coriander. Ladle into warm soup bowls, top with the remaining coriander, and serve.

As winter approaches you may have enormous parsnips left on your plot. This warming soup is an ideal use for them. Their natural sweetness is balanced by a mild curry flavour.

Curried parsnip
and apple soup

Serves 4 • **Prep** 20 mins • **Cooking** 30 mins

INGREDIENTS

1 tbsp extra virgin olive oil

10g (¼oz) butter

½ Spanish onion,
    finely chopped

1 garlic clove, crushed

2 tsp mild curry powder

1kg (2¼lb) parsnips, chopped

sea salt and freshly ground
    black pepper

1 large Bramley apple, peeled,
    cored, and chopped

1 litre (1¾ pints) hot
    vegetable stock, or
    light chicken stock

6 tbsp single cream

2 tbsp lemon juice

METHOD

1 Heat the oil and butter in a large sauté pan over gentle heat. Add the onion, garlic, and curry powder, and sweat gently, stirring frequently, for 2–3 minutes or until the onion has softened. Add the parsnips and season lightly with salt and pepper. Turn up the heat a little and fry, stirring frequently, for 5 minutes or until the parsnips are golden.

2 Add the apple, stir for 1 minute, then pour in the stock and bring to a boil. Lower the heat and simmer for 10–12 minutes or until the parsnips are tender. Take off the heat and leave to cool for several minutes, then transfer to a blender or food processor, and whizz until smooth and creamy.

3 Pass the soup through a sieve placed over the pan, then rinse out the blender or food processor with 100ml (3½fl oz) hot water and stir this into the soup. Reheat gently, then stir in the cream and lemon juice. Adjust the seasoning and serve piping hot.

PARSNIPS

When to eat
Pick baby parsnips as required. Larger parsnips are ready to be picked when the leaves die back, but will have a sweeter flavour picked after the first frosts.

Eat and store fresh
Store in the fridge for up to 1 week, or in a cool, dry place for up to 2 weeks. Parsnips can also be stored in the soil in boxes (see pages 268–9), or clamped until needed (see pages 140–1).

How to preserve
Use parsnips for home brewing or as an ingredient in chutneys.

Freezing options
Freeze as a cooked purée and keep for up to 9 months.

INDEX

ACKNOWLEDGEMENTS

Picture credits

All images © Dorling Kindersley.
For further information see www.dkimages.com.
Except: 270 (tl), 272–3: © Rough Guides; 53, 55, 56: Foodcollection RF © Getty

Dorling Kindersley would like to thank

Luis Peral for his art direction at the photoshoot, Jane Lawrie for her food styling, and Sue Rowlands for her props styling; Tessa Bindloss and Nicola Erdpresser for design help; Claire Bowers and Romaine Werblow for picture research; Anna Burges-Lumsden and Jan Fullwood for recipe testing; Sue Morony for proofreading; Liz Cook for indexing.

Caroline Bretherton's acknowledgements

My thanks go to all at Dorling Kindersley, for giving me such a joy of a project. To my parents, at whose respective knees I learnt the gentle arts of gardening and cooking. Also, to my husband, who has tirelessly consumed and appreciated almost everything I've ever cooked, as well as being a source of much encouragement. To Gabriel and Isaac, who are learning to eat most of what we grow with little fuss. Finally, thanks must go to the Acton Gardening Association, whose gift of an allotment has given me untold pleasure over the years.